# APPLIQUÉ STYLE

✳

# APPLIQUÉ
# STYLE

*

# JULIET BAWDEN

CASSELL

*For Cecilie and Thomas Blytt Mietle*

This edition first published in the UK 1997 by
CASSELL
Wellington House, 125 Strand, London, WC2R 0BB

Text copyright © Juliet Bawden 1997
Volume copyright © Cassell 1997

Distributed in the United States by Sterling Publishing Co. Inc.
387 Park Avenue South, New York, NY 10016–8810, USA

Illustrations by Kate Simunek
Designer Bet Ayer
Editor Rachel Rogers

British Library Cataloguing-in-Publication Data
A catalogue record for this book is available from the British Library

ISBN 0-304-34769-8

Typeset in Garamond
Printed and bound in Spain by Bookprint S.L.

**PICTURE CREDITS**
Karen Bell 64, 65; Jane Bristow 26, 27; Jane Burch Cochran 28, 29;
Belinda Downes c/o Methuen Childrens Books 6, 22 (top right), 32, 33, 34, 35; Ron Erickson 36, 37;
Michael Faeder 66; Deborah Gonet 38, 39; Jane A. Sassaman 22 (bottom right), 61, 62, 63.

# CONTENTS

✳

Inspired by 'I saw Three Ships Come Sailing In on Christmas Day in the Morning', an old English Christmas carol.

# INTRODUCTION

✳

Appliqué has existed for centuries. There are many books about it, some prescriptive, others more experimental, and indeed, this is not my first book on the subject. It is a decoration that is growing ever more popular both commercially, with the increasing sales of ready-made items, and as a craft, for people to express their own creativity. Many shops now carry ranges of appliquéd goods and this perhaps reflects a general need to own hand-made and personalized items almost as if to retreat from the industrial age in which we find ourselves at the turn of the millennium. Sometimes the range in the shops is small and is made by an individual artist; sometimes the work is designed in the West but carried out in the East, where unfortunately the cost of labour is cheaper.

There are now many new artists working in this medium creating fine art pieces and artefacts, and employing diverse styles and methods of working. Several of those chosen for this book have never had their work published before. What has drawn me, and I hope will you, to their work is its contemporary feel and the commitment to the design and making processes. This is reflected in the wonderful finished pieces.

The book includes both ideas and working practices. There are fifteen projects for you to copy and make, or to inspire you to create your own designs.

*Juliet Bawden*

# ORIGINS OF APPLIQUÉ

✳

The dictionary definition of appliqué is the 'decoration or trimming of one material sewn or otherwise fixed onto another'. The most obvious example is a leather patch covering a tear or hole on the elbow of a sweater or the knee of a pair of trousers. This technique of stitching one textile to another has been used for thousands of years. In ancient times, before cloth was produced in the way we know it today, skins and furs from animals were used as the material to which elaborate designs were applied; felt, feathers, stones, leaves and clay beads were sewn on with animal hair.

Although we know that appliqué has been practised for such a long time, there is very little physical evidence because of the fragility of the materials. The earliest work in existence dates from 980 BC and is thought to be a ceremonial canopy made with the dyed hide of a gazelle. The Ancient Egyptians wrapped mummified animals in appliquéd cloth and the tomb of Tutankhamen contained an appliquéd linen collar, made almost three thousand years ago. The cattle-breeding tribes of the Gobi Desert practised felt appliqué as early as 200 BC. A little later, between then and AD 200, the graves of nomadic tribes in Asia have been found to contain tents, carpets and saddle covers with designs appliquéd onto them.

The sixth century AD was when a type of appliqué called *kittsuke* was being produced in Japan. This form of embroidery, which has its origins in China and Korea, was usually used only on high class works and it took the form of figures stitched in gold and silver which were then placed over padding and attached to the background cloth.

By the Middle Ages, appliqué designs had taken on religious or symbolic meanings, hence the recurrence of particular symbols such as the cross or spiral. Ecclesiastical and military clothing, as well as banners, were appliquéd. Still today, bishops and other ecclesiastical figures have appliquéd crosses on their robes.

A general scarcity of fabrics in medieval times meant that pieces of cloth were cut from old, worn-out materials and sewn onto stronger backgrounds. This conserved the more expensive and thus rarer fabrics. Pieces of valuable cloth were used as substitutes for embroidery, which was a very important and popular pastime. Throughout Europe, appliqué was found on household items such as furniture, wall-hangings, coverlets and curtains. Sumptuous designs were produced for the richer houses and palaces; wall-hangings made by Bess of Hardwick, the Countess of Shrewsbury, can be seen today at Hardwick Hall in Derbyshire.

Appliqué in the seventeenth and eighteenth centuries manifested itself mainly in the form of quilts. Quilts are often associated with North America where, at the beginning of the eighteenth century, quilting was thought of as a social accomplishment. The American quilt-making tradition started in the seventeenth century with the arrival of British settlers. Until 1826, it was illegal for colonists to produce textiles or to buy materials from any country other than Britain. This was decreed to protect British trade monopolies. The patchwork quilt was born because the lack of equipment necessary to make good cloth meant reusing pieces of fabric from worn garments or furnishings.

*The six wives of Henry VIII* is created using the stumpwork technique, which involved padding out shapes before applying them to material to create a raised image. Stumpwork was one of the earliest forms of appliqué to be used in Britain.

Appliqué patterns on quilts were varied. One common practice was to use a large format with a design similar to a painting. Once completed, this was repeated until there were enough pieces to be joined together to make the required size. Another method was to use a smaller motif, repeat it and make it into blocks which were then joined in various ways. Quilts were made not only for warmth but also in order to give designs a three-dimensional effect. To emphasize the latter, the appliquéd motif was sometimes stuffed with wadding.

The introduction in the seventeenth century of chintz to the British market from India and from there, via smuggling, to North America, brightened and made ever more popular the art of quilt-making. Chintz is a printed cotton fabric with a glazed finish and is decorated with patterns – large birds, exotic plants and people. An appliqué technique known as *broderie perse* was often employed – this entailed applying the motifs onto a solid background. The effect was that of instant embroidery.

Album quilts appeared in America in the 1840s. They were made by groups of friends or relations who would each construct a block using appliqué. Each block would illustrate a picture or verse with the maker's signature and all would then be joined together and presented to the recipient in memory of the makers. This technique was called *cretonne appliqué* in the Baltimore area of Maryland.

The eighteenth century witnessed the use of geometrical designs from architectural masterpieces. For example, the people of Azerbaijan decorated their prayer rugs and other pieces of work thus. Also in the eighteenth century, and the nineteenth as well, the Mochis of Kutch, a part of Gujarat in India, were embroidering silver and gold chain stitch onto leathers which had been coloured red, green or black. In fact, this particular type of appliqué had originated in the late sixteenth century with Muslim craftsmen.

By the nineteenth century, the enthusiasm for appliqué had spread to the French, who called it *broderie appliqué*. It was more complicated than other forms because the first stage required gluing the fabric to thin paper and then compressing this to extract air bubbles. A design would then be drawn onto paper and cut out before being glued onto the background material. The edges of the glued material would then be finished with satin stitch or piping.

At the same time in Britain, the form of appliqué known as inlay work was becoming very popular. This method was normally used to reproduce favoured and historical prints. Each piece of cloth has to be cut and butted together precisely to hold all the oversewing carried out from the back. Purely decorative stitches were then applied to the front of the work. See pages 90–93 for more precise details of how to carry out inlay work.

Jester, sailor and soldier fabric dolls decorated with appliqué and dating from the 1950s.

Nineteenth-century literature and paintings document the fashion for appliqué and illustrate the favoured subjects – fruit and flowers in baskets and vases. These were then set in deep frames made specially to enhance the three-dimensional effect. There is a certain similarity about the designs which suggests that appliqué kits were available which included the ready-cut felt.

Manufacturers were quick to take advantage of this craze for needlework. They produced tempting novelties such as beads, sequins, braids, ribbons and threads in a wide range of colours. Felt, particularly suited to appliqué, became available in many colours and was sold in conveniently sized packages. Pattern books were printed and in the 1850s, the domestic sewing machine was invented. From then on, work could be produced with more regular stitching and at a greater speed.

The Arts and Crafts Movement started in the 1850s and included writers, painters, architects and designers. William Morris, Philip Webb, Ford Maddox Brown, Edward Burne-Jones – all were keen to use needlework techniques in their furniture and textile designs. Charles Rennie Mackintosh and M. H. Baillie Scott collaborated with their wives when experimenting with modern themes in their own homes. The Arts and Crafts Movement was successful in influencing people to change their attitudes about colour and design and made a marked contrast to the cluttered styles of Victoriana.

There was a move to take needlework to the people. In 1903, Baillie Scott wrote an article on 'the place of needlework in the house', in which he provided decorating ideas for all the family, whatever their ability. In 1906, in another article, Francis Newbery encouraged beginners to experiment with needlework and other traditional skills in the home. Newbery feared that without such encouragement, these skills would be stifled by the age of the machine. His wife, Jessie Rowat, extolled the virtues of simplicity and proposed that it was not necessary to use the most complicated designs and stitches to produce the finest examples of needlework, particularly appliqué. In 1932 the Victoria & Albert Museum held an exhibition of needlework. There were demonstrations by leading embroiderers who explained appliqué, quilting and other techniques and on the whole demystified the art.

The Second World War meant a shortage of supplies of many items including the materials necessary for various embroidery techniques. This created another innovative period in appliqué design which showed how imaginative people really can be. Fabrics never before considered were used – worn out furnishings, old coats and dresses and black-out material. Soldiers recovering from injuries took up the needle during their convalescence and found this art form to be most therapeutic.

Today, appliqué is still practised worldwide, although not quite with the fervour of the Victorians who covered just about every household item with it – cushions, teatowels, fire screens and so on. Today it is more of an art form and is produced purely for decorative purposes rather than being used for domestic items. While the techniques have changed very little, the availability of materials and the approach to design are considerably broader. Having said this, however, it must be remembered that in the poorer, less industrialized countries, the art form flourishes and traditional designs are still produced. In Hungary, for example, the *kodmon* is the most precious garment a woman can possess. It is made from appliquéd pieces which are brightly coloured when worn by a young girl but rendered more subdued when worn by an older woman. A *szur* is a man's coat which was traditionally embroidered but with the introduction of the sewing machine in the latter half of the nineteenth century, appliqué became the favoured form of decoration. Romanians still appliqué many articles of clothing such as jackets, shirts and waistcoats. These are worn for warmth, especially by those who live in the mountainous areas of the country. The Portuguese and the Spanish national costumes are also well known appliquéd garments.

In Africa the art of appliqué is found traditionally in two forms. The first is most commonly seen in southern and eastern Africa and uses beads applied to belts, bangles and head decorations. In other regions appliqué is seen on banners and flags. It is also associated with social position and power and is thus included on ceremonial robes and headwear. The Fon people of Dahomey (Benin) make colourful wall-hangings. The men spin the cotton and use bold colours for the motifs of people, mythological symbols and animals against a black background.

The most available examples of traditional appliqué are produced today in India and Pakistan. Clothes and accessories – hats, bags, belts and scarves – are appliquéd for the Western market. In Pakistan there is a technique called *shisha* which uses small pieces of mirror embroidered onto a fabric background. The many regions of Asia have a variety of techniques with specific names when applied to

Thai bag made from a patchwork of old appliqué pieces in rich mauves and purples.

*Four winds* man's hat from Lapland, made from blue wool with an appliquéd ribbon design. The utilitarian boots and muff are made from very thick felt appliquéd with brightly coloured strips of felt.

certain items. *Khatwa* is the term used when appliqué is applied to tents and canopies by the Bihar for their ceremonies; it takes the form of animals, flowers and trees. A *pichwai* is the name given to an embroidered cloth hanging in Hindu temples depicting the god Srinathji. In Gujarat, appliqué is used on domestic items and is based on a patchwork style where patterned and brightly coloured cloth is cut in a variety of sizes and sewn onto a plain background. In the Jaisalmer area, women like to appliqué everything possible, using dark, earthy colours and geometric designs.

The circle is the main decorative element in Afghanistan. Dark colour schemes with patterns picked out in turquoise, blue or white characterize the work. The *gul* is a circular cotton patch appliquéd with beads sewn in rosette patterns until the original fabric is completely covered. The patch is then applied to the garment or accessory into which small round mirrors have been incorporated.

In Central and South America, traditional textile techniques have almost always been applied to clothing. Panamanian appliqué is made by cutting a design from the background cloth and placing a piece of contrasting material behind it. This is the reverse appliqué technique – see pages 86–88. Appliqué has proved to be a valuable source of income for poorer communities who can sell their household items, hangings and clothing to tourists. Recently, the *arpillera*, which is a wall-hanging from Peru, has become a collector's item. The work depicts scenes from everyday life portrayed in minute detail, from the vegetables sold in the market to washing hanging on the line and children playing in the dusty yards. The technique originated in Chile, although there the subject matter usually carries political overtones and scenes from shanty towns are prominent.

Finally, the work of the Native Americans must not be forgotten. Nowadays, appliqués by various groups of Native Americans are produced for sale and may take the form of wall-hangings with images that often reflect the daily activities of the tribes. They originally used appliqué to decorate their clothing, shoes, belts and pouches. The base materials were seal skin, leather and canvas. Motifs often seen on totem poles have been adapted by the Native American women for use in their weaving and other applied fabric designs.

*Below:* Appliqué wall-hanging based on medieval illuminated manuscripts. The figures are hoeing and gathering and preparing food.

# INSPIRATION AND DESIGN

✳

This book is full of contemporary designers, each of whom talks about what it is that inspires them and how they go about designing. It may be the colour and texture of fabrics which inspire, or there may be certain themes and subjects which have such an emotional impact that they generate a yearning to express them in the most creative way. For the person approaching appliqué for the first time the whole concept of design and how to go about it can be rather daunting.

*Above:* Design from sketchbook ideas to finished felt scarf: playing cards with a heart motif are arranged and rearranged; stitches and embellishments are added to decorate the completed piece.

*Right:* A patchwork of what appear to be almost unrelated shapes are rearranged, appliquéd and embellished until a complete picture emerges.

Piles of brightly coloured fabrics are tightly packed on shelves. Often their random placing inspires ideas.

We are constantly bombarded with sources of design, although we may not always see them as such. Museums are full of visual references; for example, the Victoria & Albert Museum in London. This includes artefacts from many countries and different periods of history. There are departments for ceramics, costume, textiles, musical instruments, locks and keys, weapons and furniture to name but a few. Each of these departments is a rich source of design inspiration. It may be the form, the pattern or the colour which you decide to portray in your work; you may take only one element or all three to make up your own composition. Museums of natural history, with the wonderful plumage of birds and the interesting patterns on butterfly and moth wings, are yet more inspiration. Art galleries, antique shops, zoos, gardens – all can be starting points for a design.

Books, magazines, postcards and any other printed matter are sources of colour and pattern. Some of the best ideas come from the common or everyday experiences in life. For example, a bread shop full of cakes and buns, or a greengrocer's or fishmonger's shop; all these make pleasing compositions. A detail of the way the scales form patterns on a fish or the mottled surface of a pear may be the 'design trigger'. A collection of shells, a vase of flowers, brightly coloured 1930s china, old beads, pieces of embroidery: any of these may stimulate your imagination.

Once you have found your inspiration, the act of designing need not be daunting. The best designs are usually a combination of experimentation and of knowing when to stop. Very few artists will make a plan and stick to it rigidly, but they continue to experiment and work and rework until they feel they have achieved a pleasing result.

Colour is very important and may reflect mood, interest and early visual experiences. Notice how babies and children appear to have little or no taste and always go for the brightest and most garish toys.

The inspiration for a design may be the simplest of flowers. Clever manipulation of different materials – from the finest organza to thick felts – placed in layers can produce an unusual brooch or a distinctive button or even a unique hand-bound book.

These exquisite shoes show that appliqué need not be two dimensional. Based on a marine theme, the front of each shoe is formed into the shape of a sea creature.

The colours that you choose for a piece will often dictate the success of a piece of work. People on first arrival to northern Europe from hot climates, where pure and vibrant colours are part of everyday life, are surprised by the soft and subtle colours and tones of the landscapes in countries such as Belgium or Britain. Many artists and designers take their colours from nature. I once heard the late Jean Muir, the fashion designer, describing Scotland at Christmas – the clear, white, crisp snow on the ground and the sharp contrast of the red holly berries inspired her next collection. Kaffe Fassett described the impact of colour on his arrival in England from California in 1964: 'It was glowing autumn – my favourite time of year – and London was bathed in a warm pinky-gold light.'

The way in which the artists profiled approach their work is very varied. Some keep a sketchbook or doodle pad and notebook with them all the time; others like to make photographic records; others work directly from visual reference. They may work

directly with fabric and a pair of scissors, placing pieces on a background and building up a picture, adding and subtracting different pieces until a balanced composition is achieved. Or they may do the same with paper pattern pieces, which they then draw round with tailor's chalk to mark the position of each shape until the fabric is pinned into place.

If you have the use of a Polaroid camera, an interesting way of working is to place the design elements in position and take a photograph. Rearrange the various component articles, maybe even changing the background colour, and then rephotograph and repeat as many times as you wish. This process can also be done under a photocopier. Compare the photographs and use the composition that pleases you most for your final piece of work. Remember that if mistakes are made they can always be cut out, unpicked or covered up. You may find that working on more than one piece at a time is helpful, so you can pin and unpin, replace and move around pieces that please you.

The original sketch or photograph may not translate directly into the medium of appliqué and you may need to simplify the drawing or use only one section of it. Your work may not necessarily be representational. A texture or pattern may have been your initial inspiration: the paint peeling off a fence, rusty girders or flock wallpaper in an Indian restaurant.

Scale is another important aspect of design. You may wish to enlarge a design and here you will find a photocopier a useful tool – it can enlarge and reduce designs and make repeats.

Remember, when composing your work, what it is going to be used for. If it is to be made into a garment, do not put the most interesting details under the seams. Remember to leave enough border to mount your work if making a picture.

*Right:* Old photographs from the artist's family are the inspiration behind this piece of work. The images are silk screened onto canvas and appliquéd onto a plain background.

Sketches of farmyard animals and ideas about how to use them to decorate scarves.

Start a collection of fabrics, not necessarily new ones. This is a good opportunity to recycle old clothes and textiles you no longer use or need. Remember you do not have to use the fabrics as you find them; you can treat them with natural and synthetic dyes, paint, batik, tie-dye or bleach them. You can use knitted, woven or felted fabrics. It is a good idea to have a means of storing fabrics in an orderly fashion, keeping either different weights or colours together to avoid the feeling of hunting through a bag of rubbish every time you wish to start working on a new project.

Your work does not have to be stitched: many appliqué artists work using mainly fusible webbing or glue, with little or no stitching. Sometimes the stitching is purely decorative. Many combine hand sewing and machine embroidery. Nor does the appliqué have to be made up entirely of fabric:

interesting buttons, sequins, beads, tassels and lace, as well as found objects such as shells, bits of sea-smoothed bone, glass, dried seaweed or flowers may all be added to help complete a picture. Build up layers of fabric, some transparent, to give a feeling of depth to the composition.

Whatever you choose to appliqué, it will be whatever you make it. I hope I have made it clear that any material and any style and any method of working is the right one for you. The projects in this book illustrate just a few of the many combinations of design and materials – there are hundreds more combinations out there waiting to be made by you.

*Right:* Different coloured silks are bonded with fusible webbing onto a plain background. The motifs are placed on top and the whole design is then machine stitched.

# DESIGNERS AT WORK

※

Petra Boase

Jane Bristow

Jane Burch Cochran

Jo Cranston

Belinda Downes

Nancy Erickson

Deborah Gonet

Rachael Howard

Barbara Jepson

Abigail Mill

Madelaine Millington

Anne Morgan

Helen Musselwhite

Nancy Nicholson

Kate Peacock

Freddie Robins

Jane A. Sassaman

Robin Schwalb

Hayley Smith

Lisa Vaughan

Kirsten Watts

# PETRA BOASE

Petra Boase gained a BA degree in embroidery in 1993 at Manchester Metropolitan University where her degree collection was based on naïve English seaside artefacts. Today she creates mainly cushions, bags and pictures. Her work is bright and bold with strong imagery. In fact, it could be said that coloured fabrics to her are what paints are to an artist's palette.

She employs textured fabrics in her art and finds them much more effective than paints. While she is a very good painter, she is frustrated by the flatness of paint; so much more can be applied to a fabric picture. It is as if she uses a needle as her brush and if she cannot find the fabric she wants, she creates it by dyeing others.

Simple objects influence her, such as food packaging, and on a recent trip to Vietnam she was particularly inspired by the intensity of colour of the plastics in the markets. The Fauvist period in art, which used bright colours and simplified forms and is epitomized by the works of Matisse and Vlaminck, is further motivation for Petra. She is constantly look-ing for new sources for her work and finds many in her extensive travels – to Vietnam, Africa, Australia and Hong Kong.

As her work has developed since her degree, she has started using more buttons, beads and lettering. One of her first purchases for work was a new Pfaff sewing machine but she tends not to use it much as her work is more hand orientated and she feels the machine makes things look manufactured and less spontaneous. She has more recently been working in media other than textiles – children's craft books and 'makes' for magazines. The brightness and the images used in her work tend to gear it automatically towards a young market.

Her ideas for new pieces are conceived with a paper and pencil; she is a fanatic doodler and always has a sketchbook to hand. The doodles are adapted and developed and colours are decided upon by playing around with fabrics.

Petra has been commissioned to make cushions for *The Big Breakfast* show on British television and she has also been commissioned to make one-off, framed pieces for private clients as well as her contributions to textile books.

*See pages 98–99 for instructions on how to make an appliqué wash bag designed by Petra Boase.*

*Above:* Bright colours, simple shapes and lots of crazy embellishing characterize the work of Petra Boase. In just one piece of work, she has used sequins, fake flowers and machine embroidered labels.

*Left:* Cacti and patterns reminiscent of the 1950s are the inspiration behind this brightly coloured piece of work.

# JANE BRISTOW

Jane Bristow studied fashion design with printed textiles at Edinburgh College of Art. Appliqué was an important aspect of her work, including some pieces using fake fur and PVC. When she did her MA, appliqué and PVC featured strongly again – some garments had transparent PVC sewn one piece on top of the other, with layering in between. She also heat-treated the PVC to give it texture. Another of her fashion collections was influenced by Native Americans and incorporated appliquéd and embroidered totem poles and carvings.

Jane's main reason for loving appliqué is the independence it provides – she needs to turn to no one for assistance and can work completely alone. It gives her a freedom that other expressions of art could not provide.

She started appliquéing almost by accident. When she first began knitting on a machine, she kept making mistakes which created holes. She decided to patch the pieces up and sew other bits onto them. This was combined with wanting to make patterns and images that the machines could not do. It was in this way that Jane's appliqué style was born.

Duffel bags and purses are all appliquéd with PVC.

The influences on her work are many and varied – paintings, sculpture, architecture, and landscapes witnessed on her travels. Her layering with PVC came about from her interest in curves rather than straight lines in clothing – shaping her pattern cutting to the point where there were hardly any straight cut seams. She draws, paints, takes photographs, collects pictures and bits and pieces that she thinks are relevant, as well as writing notes. She particularly enjoys working in her sketchbooks, which often consist of little collages.

Jane starts off a design either by cutting up shapes and rearranging them until they look right or by leafing through her sketchbooks. She uses the latter method specifically when she is working on a theme. Although in the past she worked on themes a great deal, her accessories collections are more varied, with small, relating groups rather than a whole, themed collection.

Although Jane's early work was with clothes, she has recently been concentrating on her accessories collections, with bags, purses and aprons. She feels that she has now moved from her experimental stage of using PVC into utilizing it as a functional and practical material. Her colour and tone ideas have changed as well and where once her PVC work was bright and bold, now it is more subtle.

Although appliqué is a traditional craft, it is not only traditional materials that can be used. PVC has added an interesting dimension to this bag.

# JANE BURCH COCHRAN

Jane Burch Cochran's formal art training began with a major in mathematics and art and was followed by the study of painting at Cincinnati Art Academy. She was inspired to make the art quilts for which she is now renowned when she saw those of Terrie Mangat. In 1979 she began to make small fibre pieces and in 1985 she tried her first quilt. So successful was she that she now works at it full time.

Initially, she made small collages using painted canvas, photocopied transfers, fabric and beads. She beaded the collages then added fabric and images, appliquéing them onto the background with bugle and seed beads. Nowadays, the bulk of her work consists of appliquéing her patchwork pieces onto the background with beads, meaning that she does not have to turn the patchwork edges under. She likes to use articles of clothing to signify parts of the body. Gloves are an especial favourite; she feels that the symbol of the hand, encapsulated by the glove, is reaching and searching for both questions and answers about the issues of race, environment and the human psyche.

Her main influences are Victorian crazy quilts and Native American beadwork, as well as the work of the Abstract Impressionists.

Embellished with beads and sequins, this piece was inspired by the view that washing lines waving in the breeze tell many a tale about a family. The artist describes it as a self-portrait, part gypsy butterfly, part queen and part moon chaser.

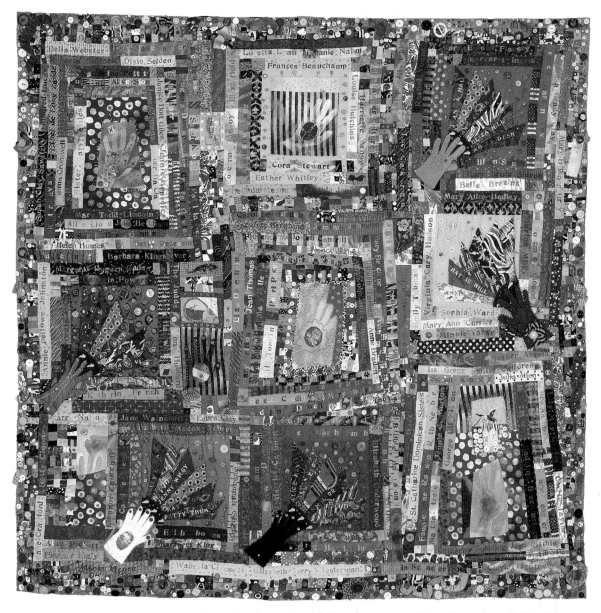

This appliqué quilt contains over 200 names of famous and not so famous Kentucky women, a history lesson in itself. It took two years to make from scraps of material sewn together, appliquéd onto a background then decorated with buttons.

Jane feels that when she is working on a patchwork, the way that she uses fabrics is like creating a small painting with cloth. A design usually starts as a visual image in her mind. She may then make some sketches or start pinning parts of the image on a wall. She collects materials and makes up pieces of patchwork and the fact that her work is so textural means that often she cannot predict the finished product until it is before her.

When making up patchworks, she cuts up random strips of material and sews them together. These are then cut up again and sewn to other strips. She then appliqués the patchwork onto the background and hides the raw edges with beads and sequins.

In 1993 Jane received a Southern Arts Federation Fellowship and an Al Smith Artist Fellowship. She now has quilts in the University of Kentucky Art Museum; she has had two solo shows and many group shows, including the 'Contemporary American Quilts' at the London Crafts Council; and numerous galleries display and sell her work. Occasionally she teaches at workshops, but ideally she likes just to work – on her patchwork and appliqué quilts and in her garden in rural Kentucky.

# JO CRANSTON

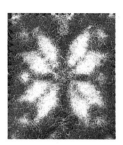

Jo Cranston produces a range of knitted felt and appliquéd fabrics and garments. She studied fashion and textiles at Brighton University where she first experimented with making knitted felt and discovered that felt does not fray and is ideal for cutting into shapes and sewing together. New possibilities were opened up to her as she knitted together lengths of patterned and multi-coloured fabrics and then washed them until all the fibres bonded to become a blanket-like fabric. This new fabric could then be cut out and appliquéd together, resulting in an almost padded or quilted effect. So special was it that people could not guess how the fabric was made.

*Above:* Two-colour machine knitted and felted appliqué scarf. The fish are knitted, felted and then sewn on top of the scarf.

*Left:* An appliqué sampler which uses traditional fairisle flower motifs, patterns and colours. The pieces are knitted separately on a machine then patched and appliquéd together.

Jo feels that her artistic family background and the constant support and encouragement she received was very influential. It enabled her to be confident enough to establish herself as a sole trader in 1992, to be accepted onto the Enterprise Allowance Scheme and so to buy a knitting machine and a stock of yarns. Her business has been growing steadily, from one initial order from Paul Smith to exhibiting at Britain's premier knitwear show, 'Design in Knitwear', which brought in many international orders and commissions. She now exports felted and appliquéd waistcoats, scarves and hats to Hong Kong, America, Japan and France.

She has been influenced by many things, both people, animals and natural objects: her mother's embroidery and dressmaking; the Ndebele women of Zimbabwe and their beautiful red, yellow and blue felted blankets for weddings and ceremonies; leaves, fish, and animal skins, which are vividly illustrated on her garments and blankets.

She feels she is always at work, designing in her head or jotting down ideas in her notebook. She is inspired by the colours people wear or food in a supermarket – her 1995 collection was based on fish, including trout, mackerel and plaice. She certainly knew the fish extremely well by the time she had finished her collection – the initial designs began as detailed drawings of the fish and close up photographs capturing the subtle variety of colours.

# BELINDA DOWNES

Belinda took a BA degree in embroidery at Loughborough College of Art and Design. She produces pieces of appliqué which are then photographed and used as illustrations. She had always enjoyed drawing and latterly painting and wanted to manipulate thread and fabric in the same way. For years she felt frustrated with her unsatisfactory results – she wanted to paint on paper and then embroider a similar image, capturing at the same time something new because of the quality of the fabric and thread. Her appliqué designs grew out of the need to be able to add colour or an image to her fabric background. She would lay down pieces of dyed or painted fabrics in shapes to recreate brush marks and then appliqué scraps of fabric, carefully chosen for their colour and texture, in different directions.

Within the last five years Belinda has become more involved with pattern and has enjoyed searching out patterns in historical embroidery. Before this, her main inspiration came from painting. The work could be from any era or culture. Both the Arts and

Initially an illustration for a greeting card, this picture portrays Holly and Ivy as great friends dressing up for an evening out.
The main bodies and faces are appliquéd while the details are machine and hand embroidered.

The background cotton fabric was painted with fabric dye to give a cloudy sky. The shapes of angels and shepherds were then applied and the details added with embroidery silks and hand embroidery stitches, including couching, satin stitch, French knots and stab stitches. The angels' gowns were inspired by Bulgarian and Hungarian costume embroidery.

Crafts Movement and the Bloomsbury set are strong influences. They allowed arts and crafts to go hand in hand, so that pattern can stand alongside fine art. The result is a powerful mix of objects and pictures.

When making an embroidery Belinda constantly thinks about composition, blocks of colour and interest within a piece, leading the eye up and down, around and across the embroidered surface. She likes to use both hand and machine embroidery and particularly to free machine embroider with straight stitch to fill in areas with colour.

*Left:* Based upon the movement of early settlers to America, this scene of a boy and a girl watching ships used lengths of gold and silver thread and strips of blue fabric layered beneath transparent nylon to create a wavy sea. The fish were directly influenced by seventeenth-century stumpwork fish, which were simple and stylized. Both hand- and machine-stitched embroidery was used.

The padded cherubic statue in the foreground is covered in layers of long straight stitch. The background and garden were built up first by appliquéing scraps of dyed fabric to represent the brush marks of a painting, then with hand-stitched decoration to represent herbs and flowers.

A Christmas scene of appliquéd angels flying over stables on small panels of dark green cotton. The couples, hearts and shepherds were inspired by German folk art and carvings. The work is embellished with different embroidery stitches and highlighted with gold thread. The entire piece has been put together as stained glass appliqué, with red ribbon as the leading.

Her early work reflected her interest in painted landscape and figures and historical embroidery (mainly of the sixteenth and seventeenth centuries). It sometimes told stories of gods and goddesses, planetary movements and Zodiac signs. She would dye fabrics to suit her paintings and redraw the picture outline onto stretched white cotton She would then add dyed shapes, appliquéing by hand to represent the brush marks. Figures were usually padded – wadding would be cut or manipulated into shapes and stitched down quickly, then covered with muslin and layers of coloured thread.

Today Belinda works more quickly. She is constantly sketching and doodling, and keeps everything as a source of material for finished pieces. She does not plan as accurately as she used to and allows herself to be guided by the initial subject idea but is then led by fabric surfaces and patterns. She still pads her figures and faces.

Her work is sold through exhibitions and her embroideries are to be used for greetings cards, books and advertising. She has made large hangings for shopping arcades. She has taught day and weekend courses and workshops for both adults and children and is occasionally a visiting lecturer for degree courses.

# NANCY ERICKSON

Nancy is a fine artist who has quite a few qualifications under her belt – a BA degree in zoology, an MS degree in foods and nutrition, an MA in painting and an MFA in painting and drawing. Textiles and fibres were not really an option educationally in America and so when she was asked to do some extra sculptures credits for her MFA, she made them out of fabric. They were large, dyed and painted amorphous shapes, intended as friendly pieces for children to lean and sit on.

Nancy works in fabric as it is so versatile that it can be cut, printed, painted or stuffed, and she loves the various qualities, especially those of satin, velvet and cotton. Her works are large quilted pieces, consisting of the various fabrics appliquéd onto shaped backgrounds.

During the Gulf War Nancy put aside working on fabric and concentrated on oil pastels on paper. When she came back to fabric, she began to paint directly onto the material within a rectangular shape, working more freely as if she were working on paper. She then layers the pieces and stitches them on her sewing machine.

A background in fine art is apparent in her designs and the patterns and formats of her appliquéd work derive from her own paintings. Currently, she likes to draw a number of sketches to try out various forms. She pins the fabric on the wall so that she can study it clearly and then she starts drawing directly onto the fabric before painting over it. When she has gone as far as she can go with the paint, Nancy starts adding the appliqué fabrics. For this stage, she uses an industrial sewing machine. When the main bulk of the painting and appliqué work is done, she lines the fabric with polyester and then tacks on another backing, making the polyester the middle piece. However, Nancy finds her methods changing with each piece that she does and does not stick to a specific routine.

Nancy is, in the strictest sense, a fine artist and so it is her drawings for which she is best known and which are readily available on the market. Her fabric pieces are more unusual, being larger and often figurative, and are a distinctive expression of the less conventional side of a fine artist at work.

*Left:* The artist's love of both paint and fabric is apparent in this depiction of a figure at the bottom of the stairs beside a proud lion.

Painted canvas has been appliquéd with silks, satins and velvet to create a collage of tactile pieces.

# DEBORAH GONET

After graduating in embroidered and woven textiles, Deborah went on to to do an MA in the same subject. Although she enjoyed both disciplines, she realized in the final year of her MA that embroidery was her true love; she is excited by the immediacy with which one can transform a plain piece of fabric into something rich and beautiful. Since colour, pattern and texture are so important in Deborah's work, she finds that appliqué is an ideal medium for their translation into fabric and stitch. She likes to choose interesting background fabrics and decorate and embellish them. She uses this technique to decorate her waistcoats, cushions, quilts and wall-hangings.

Two designers who influence Deborah are Elsa Schiaparelli and Christian Lacroix – their sense of design and use of colour in their lavishly embellished garments are what fire her imagination. But she is also inspired by nature, landscapes, aerial views and decorative art, including wrought ironwork and jewellery. The paintings of artists Hundertwasser, Sonia Delauney, Rossetti, Klimt and Klee play major roles in Deborah's work as well.

When she is working on a range of designs or a project, Deborah will go to museums, exhibitions, libraries and bookshops, seeking out materials for her ideas. She sketches and takes photographs of things that catch her eye. She builds up a collection of sketches, photographs, postcards, books and magazine cuttings, which she pins on boards and lays out in front of her to allow it all to soak in. From these she designs waistcoats and cushions, for example,

These heavily appliquéd waistcoats are made with rich fabrics such as satin, velvet and silk to achieve an almost quilted effect. The motifs are essentially simple but once stitched together look intricate.

This floral waistcoat uses reverse and shadow appliqué to give the flowers an almost three-dimensional look, especially when combined with the light background.

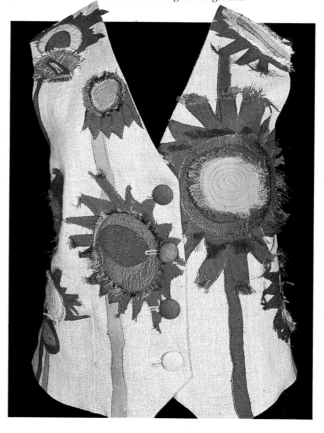

The very rich fabrics in jewel-like colours give these cushions maximum impact.

onto layout paper. She starts in black and white and adds elements, colours and patterns that she finds interesting. The main colour is not decided upon until she starts working with the fabric.

Silk in its many forms is one of her favourite fabrics because of its feel and draping qualities. Linens are used for their tactile qualities and velvets for their elegance and luxuriance. Deborah uses rayon embroidery threads for the stitches because they have a very lustrous quality and come in many colours.

Deborah's earlier work consisted of both weaving and embroidery and was mainly about colour and texture. It was only on leaving college, when she set up her own business, that Deborah began to work in appliqué on her waistcoats. This is what she continues to do today. Exhibitions at various galleries and fairs give Deborah retailing opportunities, but her work is sold mainly to private customers. She takes on both private and public commissions. She also teaches and lectures.

# RACHAEL HOWARD

The background fabric of this cushion is screen printed with an enlarged copy of an old receipt. The chickens were applied then machine stitched for extra definition.

Rachael Howard graduated in embroidery at the Royal College of Art. She now creates wonderful appliqué ties, scarves and cushions.

In her final year at the RCA she won the Fleur Cowles Award for excellence, for which the prize was a six-week work placement at an embroidery factory in New Delhi, India. The factory exported table linen for shops like Habitat. Rachael's job involved making patchwork combinations, sampling and choosing colourways. And so India became a major source of inspiration for Rachael's work, both drawing and needlework. In fact, on her return to England, her sketches were put together into an exhibition entitled 'Visions of India' in the Voirrey Embroidery Centre in her native Merseyside.

Rachael's degree show had comprised a series of appliquéd and embroidered collages trapped between two sheets of plastic. Her method was to photocopy a set of sketches, which included drawings of visitors at Crufts and the state opening of Parliament, onto a sheet of acetate. This was then padded out by arranging pieces of fabric and loops of thread onto the bodies. Finally, this was sealed with a top layer of plastic sheeting. Once she had graduated, Rachael took a course in silk screen printing because she wanted to achieve a way of using her drawings on fabric. Now she screen prints fragments of text – often based on letters, bills and tickets – behind her appliquéd figures.

She specializes in cushions, scarves and wall hangings with quirky figures which have been appliquéd and embroidered and which have screen printed backgrounds. Working from an initial sketch,

she cuts out scraps of fabric for the bodies and clothes of her figures and then bonds them onto a cotton or linen background fabric. She then screen prints her original line drawing over the top of the bonded scraps and sews on details and shading with her sewing machine.

Rachael's cushions and scarves are sold at a number of stores, including Habitat and the Crafts Council, and she has done some tie collections for Paul Smith. However, she is keen to work on her larger wall-hangings and is currently working on a large piece based on her travels to India.

Ties from the Paul Smith Collection. From left to right, *Lady and gentleman dancing* on pink and white check, *Doves* on white linen, *Turquoise flower with buds* on pink linen and *Girl and boy with balloons* on blue, green and white check.

Inspired by a trip to India, this throw features figures observed from the artist's experiences in an Indian textile factory. The use of checked fabric cut on the bias helps to express the movement in a convincing yet understated way.

# BARBARA JEPSON

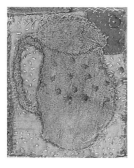

company selling knitting yarns at the same time as raising a family. As the family grew older they decided to change direction; her husband took a degree in psychology and became an infant teacher and she started a part time course in creative embroidery. After a City and Guilds course, which was technique based, Barbara decided to enrol on a foundation course and then went on to take a BA at Manchester Metropolitan University. Her work experience and her newer qualifications have enabled her to produce sumptuous compositions using blankets.

When she is working on a project, she starts by putting down layers and then cutting them away in certain areas. She will often cut up an appliquéd piece and place the parts on more spacial backgrounds.

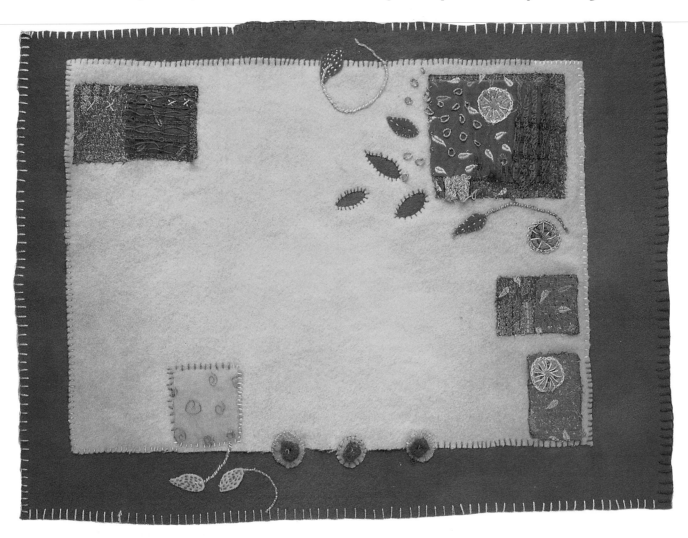

Blankets and woollen fabrics accept dyes really well and the colours often look stunning, as do the yellow and blue on this piece. To achieve a quilted look here, blanket has been appliquéd onto blanket so that the stitches sink into the surface.

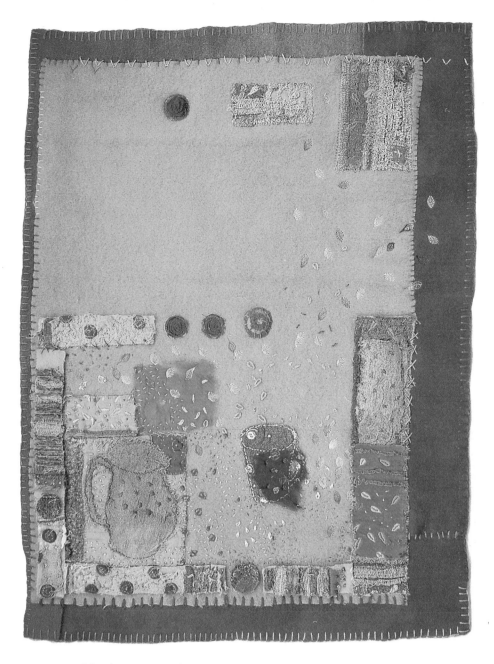

*Right:* A dyed blanket is the background material for this wonderful and vividly coloured work. Different materials were sewn on, then details added with hand stitching. Along the border, yarns are couched onto a piece of blanket and appliquéd onto the background fabric.

piece and place the parts on more spacial backgrounds. Sometimes she reapplies the cut out shapes to the base fabrics, thereby mirroring the cut back appliqué. She sews over the appliqué with hand and machine stitch to incorporate the applied fabric into the base fabric. The intensity of the colours she uses is highlighted by her choice of fabrics – raised blanket, velvet or silk organza.

For inspiration, she draws, but tends to be influenced more by the colour from the drawings than by their actual form. She therefore dyes ranges of fabrics and looks at the results for suggestions of how to build up a composition. The art of Matisse and Bonnard is important to Barbara for colours while the textiles of India shape her ideas about patterns. She likes to see how a dot or a mark travels through the different patterns unifying the whole piece. It was the use of a Pfaff sewing machine that showed her how a machine could be employed more innovatively: she found that the automatic single motif provided her with the unifying mark while the darning stitch or vermicelli stitch, when moved in different directions, created a textured surface which pushed the appliquéd fabric into the base fabric.

# ABIGAIL MILL

Abigail trained in textiles at Cumbria College of Art and Design where she discovered her love of creating textures and surfaces and layering colours. She worked out to perfection a technique that combined the three-dimensional qualities of hand-dyed felt with soft, sheer fabrics like shot silk, velvet and organza. This is the method she now works with constantly to produce her pictures and accessories.

She is inspired by decorative, jewel-like and rich sources, quoting Italian architecture and the flowers of the West Indies as her main influences, with marine animal and plant life not far behind.

After graduating, Abigail made hats as she had specialized in felt-making, millinery and embroidery whilst at college. However, she soon discovered that although she enjoyed making them, she was unable to market and sell them in the recession, as they were so elaborate and were deemed to be luxury items. Her work then changed direction as she

A selection of fabric shells and sea life made from satin and silk using trapunto and shadow work techniques.

44

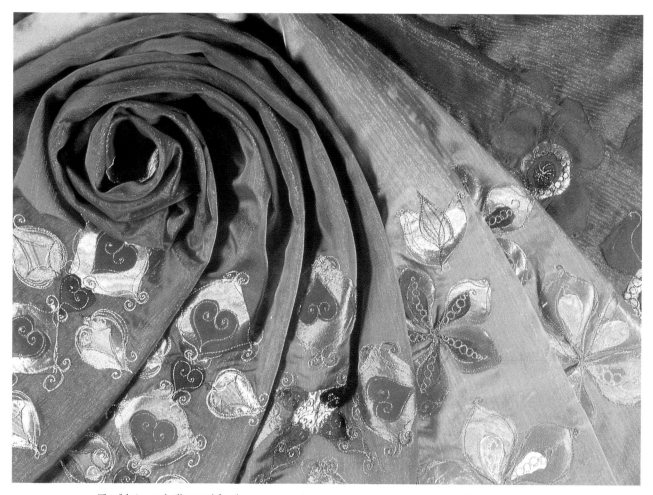

The fabrics and silks used for these scarves are extremely luxurious and are just asking to be touched.

concentrated on decorative embroidery rather than millinery. From this point, embroidered and appliquéd jewellery became the bread and butter products of her business. As these took off, her business and experience grew, and so she expanded from embroidered product lines to larger and one off pieces.

Her work is now very much in demand but the consequent pressures mean that Abigail is unable to spend as much time as she would like on designing and working on new ideas: she needs to take time out to enable her to develop her work, yet has to continue making up orders to generate a cash flow. This puts her in the position of many newly successful designers in that she has to decide which direction she would like to go in.

In the six shows that she participates in each year, Abigail sells her work directly to the public. Her work is also sold in retail outlets throughout Britain, Europe and Japan. She designs ranges of embroidery which are then published as greetings cards and also creates embroidery designs to be used as packaging.

Just after her graduation, Abigail was offered work teaching felt-making at several art schools and embroidery workshops; she continues to do this alongside her design and commercial work.

*See pages 104–105 for instructions on how to make appliqué flowers designed by Abigail Mill.*

# MADELAINE MILLINGTON

Madelaine's main subject at teacher training college was art and craft, specializing in screen printing. For twelve years she taught art to various age groups, and during this time took a City and Guilds course in embroidery. During the course, she was given a brief to do a sampler of formal and free appliqué, interpreted from her own sketches. It was when she began looking at some Indian hats for ideas that her fascination with appliqué came about; she immediately felt that she could think and interpret in this medium. This was how she wanted to work and is now how she produces her wonderful hats and waistcoats as well as pieces of fine art.

With appliqué, Madelaine has found that she can use bright colours boldly and can embellish the finished product as much or as little as she likes. It is also a handy way of recycling and reusing old scraps of material. Aspects of appliqué that she particularly enjoys are the piecing together of fabrics and the layering to make a sandwich of many different colours, some of which are then cut away to reveal the colours beneath. This gives an almost three-dimensional look to work and the thicker the fabrics, the 'crunchier' the effect.

This bird sampler uses a simple motif which has been layered using felt. Hand stitches have been added for detail as well to quilt the motif. The tail feathers consist of couched yarns.

The stumpwork technique has been used here to give the jester depth. The individual pieces were stuffed before being appliquéd onto the background. The jester's shirt and bloomers create an appliqué on appliqué.

Heralding angels in bright and boldly coloured felt. some dyed to achieve the right shades. make this pelmet a warm addition to any room.

Part of Madelaine's course involved the study of celestial bodies. With a priest for a father and a cathedral organist for a husband, Madelaine was more than familiar with such images. She looked particularly closely at the period of Opus Anglicanum – the latter half of the twelfth century when English embroidery was at a peak. The work tended to be made of very rich and luxurious fabrics, with much couching and raised work details. These embroideries and the Gothic architecture of the time influence Madelaine's work. She translated medieval spires and buildings into her work, using modern felts in bold and bright colours. Once the appliqué work has been done, she then couches in details and uses the cut back method.

Madelaine carries a small sketchbook with her at all times. When she works out a new design, she draws it in pen and then colours it. She has to decide upon the colours before she starts appliquéing because there are so many. Any embellishments are usually added as she goes along. The fabrics she uses are old blankets, wool, silk, felt and calico. She dyes the fabrics as she finds necessary. She uses perle threads for their sheen and wide colour spectrum.

*See pages 96–97 and 102–103 for instructions on how to make a chequered waistcoat and a jester's hat, both designed by Madelaine Millington.*

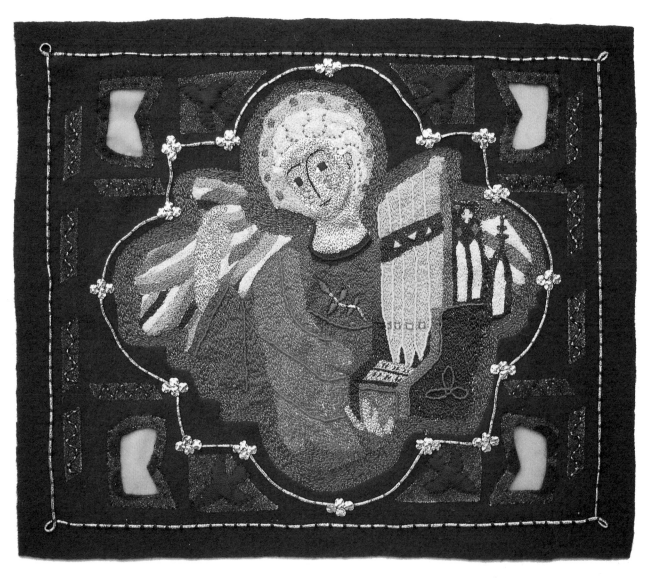

The theme of much of Madelaine's work is celestial bodies and her most commonly used fabric is felt.
This haloed angel in reverse appliqué is therefore typical of her style.

# ANNE MORGAN

Anne Morgan is following in a long family tradition – her mother and grandmother made clothes for the family and furnishings for their home; her great-grandmother was a seamstress specializing in embroidered bodices for Victorian ladies. Anne studied dressmaking at school, then made her own clothes and her children's. Embroidery began to interest her only after she saw an exhibition of embroidery at Stockport Art Gallery. She was so taken aback by the work that she felt she must try it out. This lead to her studying textiles at college and she now spends most of her days lost beneath piles of fabrics, fibres and thread creating her bags and wall-coverings.

Anne makes her own painted papers and her use of appliqué was a response to her quest for a method that would enable her to combine her papers with felts, silk and threads. Her aim is to create rich and varied effects which are layered and combined by overstitching with cut back techniques then used to reveal colours and textures beneath.

The central motif is reverse appliqué which has been detailed with hand and machine stitching. The border is painted paper appliqué.

She is influenced by African textiles – her Fante bird, for example, is based upon the flag techniques of the Asante people – and by the landscape. She takes lots of photographs; some lead into series of drawings in charcoal, pastels and acrylic, others are made into photomontages. Her sketches and paintings and her own papers, torn up and made into collages, are also sources for appliqué ideas. Her favoured fabrics are hand-dyed silks, canvas, hand-made paper, wool and silk felt of various densities. She finds it better to be imprecise about the detail of the design since she cuts and re-assembles the materials in layers to create abstract forms until she is satisfied with the result.

Anne has sold her work privately through galleries and exhibitions and recently she has been working by commission. She has given workshops, mainly in primary and secondary schools, and gives individual tutorials. She has recently joined forces with a painter friend to give a series of thematic workshops, which include appliqué techniques.

*See pages 124–125 for instructions on how to make inlay bags designed by Anne Morgan.*

Made of felt, cut back, then hand and machine embroidered, this panel was appliquéd onto a drawn thread cotton background, finished with a fringe.

# HELEN MUSSELWHITE

Helen Musselwhite is a three-dimensional designer. Her work as an appliqué artist is rather unusual in that she decorates furniture with appliqué, as well as the more regular fabric bases. Helen's art school background is actually in two-dimensional design; she studied graphics for four years which led her to work in illustration and surface design. From this point she began to work in three-dimensional design and papier maché was the medium that she began with. However, she found it too time consuming, restrictive as a medium and not cost effective for her purposes. So she started to use palette wood to make small pieces of furniture, mirrors and clocks, incorporating many different media – paints, metal foils, beads and, of course, fabrics.

Helen decorates many things with appliqué, from bedcovers and cushions to her hand-made furniture. She uses simple and practical fabrics like gingham, denim, calico, all of them either plain or dyed in strong vibrant colours.

She is influenced by the folk art of the southern Mediterranean and the vivid colours of northern India and Latin America. For further ideas, she looks through magazines and books and she visits galleries. She makes quick sketches and chooses colours, then begins working on mock-ups to get a feel for the medium she is working in and to experiment with different methods.

Her furniture is made from wood which is sanded and limed to give an attractive well worn look. She adds details with household paints and metal foils, which she embosses and cuts into shape. Finally she appliqués various details with different fabrics, sometimes mixing media by sewing fabric onto the foil, for example.

Calico, gingham and felt work especially well together because of the instant graphic effects achieved by the very different colours and textures. Helen cuts the material into the bold and simple shapes of hearts, stripes, spots and animals such as cats, dogs and fish. She either sews or glues the fabric in place and then picks out various details with large and irregular hand stitches in contrasting coloured embroidery threads.

Her work is sold through small, independent shops and galleries throughout Britain and is often featured in home interest magazines. Much of her work is actually commissioned, using her designs in colours to suit a customer's home. In the future Helen's ambition is to produce a complementary range of home accessories in wood, fabric and china.

*See pages 120–121 for instructions on how to make a gingham fish cushion designed by Helen Musselwhite.*

This naïve little clock has been appliquéd in the same manner as the *Gingham fish cushion* (see pages 120–121). The main part is felt with the face and its pompom crown hand stitched on. Once the sewing is completed, the cover is stretched over the basic clock.

# NANCY NICHOLSON

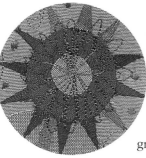

Nancy Nicholson is the daughter of textile designers. Her main influence in life has been, and still is, her mother, Joan Nicholson, who has written a number of books on embroidery. Nancy's first degree was in graphics at Maidstone College of Art. She went on to the Royal College of Art to study tapestry, and there she worked mainly in paper, fabric and wood, creating wall hangings.

Her inspirations can come from anywhere, be it a coffee cup, something in an Oxfam shop, a mother and child, artists of a certain period or movement – Patric Heron, David Hockney, Alexander Calder – 1940s and 1950s design pieces. She is particularly fascinated by children's books and their illustrations; the work of Brian Wildsmith had a great influence on her as a child and she would endlessly look through his books.

She does not have one particular design process and so the way she approaches a project depends upon its nature. On the whole, however, she uses her collection of sample fabric books, her palette of colours and a scrapbook full of ideas. The fine pictures she embroiders are very personal; she keeps a basket of silks in her work-room and picks up colours she

likes. She often works on about ten pieces at a time, perhaps connected by a theme. She sews and then appliqués the pieces and perhaps draws on top of them with hand and machine embroidery. The work develops as it evolves.

Nancy had originally worked in monochrome, printing and batiking papers to be sold. But the recession hit hard in the fine art world and Nancy took up the needle instead. It was with the birth of her children that she changed from working in monochrome to using bright and bold colours. She perceives her future direction as selling designs rather than manufacturing them, although she would like to carry on producing appliqué since she likes the hands-on approach as well as the design process for it and finds that the small size of the works she produces makes them exciting to work on. Nancy describes herself as a cutter rather than a drawer.

*See pages 116–117 for instructions on how to make buttons designed by Nancy Nicholson.*

Each cup and flower has different details appliquéd on. All have been bonded onto the background fabric with fusible webbing then machine stitched, partly to keep them in place but primarily to decorate them.

*Above:* To make this flower and leaf in a mug, silk scraps have been bonded onto the background fabric with fusible webbing and the details have been sewn on with a machine using free stitched circles and lines.

*Above:* Each plain square has simple appliquéd motif and each edge has little triangular banners, making this a charming patchwork quilt.

*Below:* Flora and fauna are a constant source of inspiration for Nancy. Here the squares have been bonded together with fusible webbing so that the result looks similar to a patchwork, then flowers and leaves have been stitched on in a glorious array of colour.

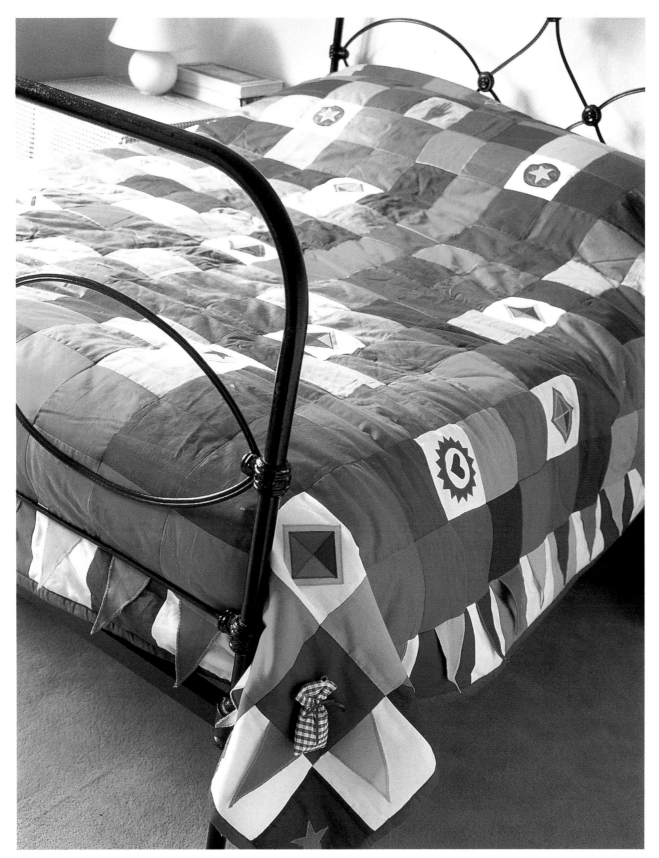

This quilt has irregular coloured squares which have been appliquéd with diamond, star and heart motifs before being sewn together. The banners are triangular and each corner has a tiny drawstring bag attached.

# KATE PEACOCK

Kate Peacock studied embroidery at Manchester College of Art and graduated in 1995. The course was broad based and taught her traditional embroidery and sewing techniques as well as life drawing, experimental drawing and the study of textiles. She is currently teaching on a foundation course at Berkshire College and making samples for Designers' Guild. Her own work is in the field of fashion and household accessories.

Her ideas for the colours of her pieces come mainly from fabrics, which on the whole she dyes herself. Like almost all the designers featured in this book, Kate keeps a sketchbook permanently to hand and sketches various shapes as she sees them. When it comes to transferring her ideas onto the fabric, she does not necessarily copy the shapes directly from her sketchbooks, but somehow the general idea seems to seep in.

She studies landscapes and still life and looks for areas with different qualities that could provide shapes to make textiles. She tries to follow a line and see how it runs randomly through a piece of work. Often, her textiles are an exaggeration or an enlargement of what she sees.

At the very start of a project, the design stage, she decides upon the shape, size and colour. She then plays around with fabric pieces, laying one on another until the effect feels right to her. This layering is particularly successful with sheer fabrics, which can change the colour of other fabrics beneath them or give a shadowy effect.

To date, Kate has been asked to make some bags for the Designers' Guild and to write a book on machine embroidery. She teaches one day a week and is keen to supply designs for greetings cards and wrapping paper.

*See pages 106–107, 108–109 and 118–119 for how to make a lampshade, a hand bound book and a bag, all designed by Kate Peacock.*

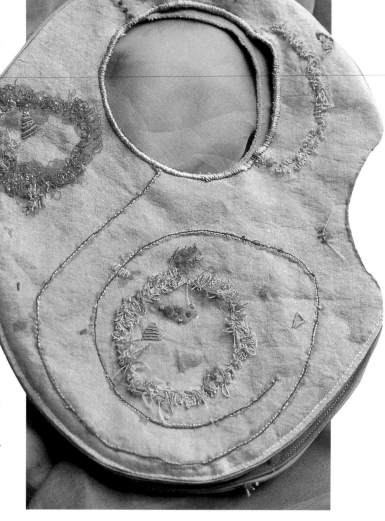

*Above:* This bag has been made in the same way as the *Pop Art bag* (see pages 118–119) with shadow appliqué and cut work used as main techniques. The delicate look is offset by bold satin stitch bordering the handles and the edge seams.

*Right:* These purses are tiny delicate pieces of art just about the right size for a lipstick; they are definitely decorative rather than functional.

# FREDDIE ROBINS

Freddie was introduced to sewing and knitting by her godmother, a fact which, she claims, probably saved her from office drudgery. She graduated from Middlesex University with a degree in textiles and fashion and then went on to the Royal College of Art to study for an MA in textile design, specializing in knitwear. After that, she teamed up with Ingrid Tait and Jacqui McLennan to form Tait and Style, a design group which produces embroidered and felted fabrics, as well as fashion and furnishing accessories.

The appliqué work that Freddie does for Tait and Style is not a traditional appliqué method for the different fabrics are not stitched onto a background cloth but instead are needle-punched or machine-felted together. This process involves the fabrics being put through a machine that has two beds of needles which 'mash' the fabric fibres together, so fusing them into one. This technique can be used only with very hairy and fibrous fabrics, which is why Freddie tends to use wool fabrics and yarns. When she wants to achieve a flat colour or a graphic effect, she uses craft felt; when she wants to outline images or to add fine details and sew on buttons for added detail, she uses wool yarn.

Freddie likes to make the ordinary extraordinary and pay homage to the overlooked and the ignored.

Thus her influences range from cows, horse cemeteries and cups of tea to medical instruments, human organs, hospitals and domestic appliances. Her work is undeniably humorous and graphic, sometimes even subversive, but at the same time, she can tailor it to suit the market.

A design can be sparked off by the slightest thing – a word, a fleeting mental image, a memory. Freddie keeps a sketchbook for her ideas and images. She often writes lists of words and names. She does not sketch out her design to start with but instead places her sketchbooks, notes, photographs and cuttings around her and begins to draw out the shapes in full size on large sheets of paper. This paper becomes the template. She then plays around with the shapes and colours until she finds an arrangement she likes.

*Left:* This beautiful throw with felt work is not, strictly speaking, appliqué. Wool motifs are cut out and attached to the background fabric by 'mashing' the motifs and background together, then steaming them so that they look like one and the same piece.

*Right:* A detail taken from a throw depicting a farmyard. The finer detail is added with a sewing machine, although the writing is couched yarn, one of Freddie's trademarks.

If a drawing of a design does exist, it is because she has drawn it afterwards as a record, and keeps it with snips of fabric, felt, yarn and written notes.

Freddie's earlier work displayed bright colours but to conform to the custom of Tait and Style her palette is now more subdued while her fabrics and images are more eclectic. By her own admission, she appreciates that not everyone wants to be as open about their opinions as her work may sometimes suggest. However, there is often a hidden message which maintains her subversive and humorous streak. These messages are disguised in traditionally patterned and coloured fabrics. For example, in a recent collection she knitted snowflake fairisles but if you look closely you can see that they are actually guns arranged in star-shaped patterns.

She is currently a visiting tutor for Textiles and Fashion at Winchester School of Art and at Buckinghamshire College. She has taught appliqué only once, when she taught a special needs class for adults with severe learning difficulties, combining machine knitting, felting (needle-punching) and appliqué to produce pieces which had coloured felt needle-punched onto machine-knitted fairisle fabrics.

Her work, especially her scarves, sells all over the world, with her main retail outlets being Liberty and Selfridges in London, Barney's in New York and many shops in Scotland, because Tait and Style are an Orkney based firm.

*See pages 110–111 for instructions on how to make a hand and eye scarf designed by Freddie Robins.*

The heart is a familiar feature in Freddie's work – this particular one was inspired by a pack of playing cards.
The motif is simple; it is the couching that gives it detail.

# JANE A. SASSAMAN

Jane graduated from Iowa State University in textile and jewellery design. She worked in many design media before discovering quilting and from that appliqué in 1980. She found that quilting or 'soft paintings' satisfied the artist, draftsperson and craftsperson in her. An added bonus was the fact that she enjoyed the design process and the actual hand work.

Most of Jane's quilts are symbolic statements about cycles and spiritual forces of life. These are expressed with the bold, graphic style and bright primary colours that make her quilts so distinctive. Each quilt starts as an idea or image that flashes through Jane's mind and which she quickly sketches in her ever handy sketchbook. Often the idea is simply a combination of colours or a proportion.

Naïve shapes and graphic colours make these appliquéd images of nature very striking. Vivid colours on dark backgrounds have machine stitches in careful rows sewn onto them. It is almost as if the machine is a paintbrush and the fabric a canvas.

There is much intricate machine quilting here as rows and rows of coloured threads are sewn from top to bottom of each appliquéd motif like a brush adding colour to a painting. Eastern European textiles are the inspiration behind the image.

The next stage is to cut shapes in random fabrics to play around with. The cutting out gives her negative shapes as well, from the pieces that she has cut and removed, so she constantly gets new, unexpected shapes. If she is working on a larger piece, however, more planning is needed. She makes an initial sketch then makes full size images and transfers them to a master pattern. She then rearranges them until she is happy with the result.

Jane calls herself a 'design sponge' as she is constantly tuned into shapes and designs that surround her. She is particularly drawn to American and

*Left:* Inspired by nature and with heraldic emblems and motifs, this piece has a regal appearance yet still manages to look naïve with its bright and bold colours.

European art movements from the 1850s to the 1920s, from the Pre-Raphaelites to the Vienna Secession.

Although she occasionally works to commission, she only does so if it will advance her current work. The colours are very important and Jane must be able to relate to them on a piece of work. Apart from this, Jane does sell a fair amount of work, through both private and public collections. Individual collectors tend to buy the smaller pieces as they are more affordable and domestic in size.

Jane has exhibited her quilts for many years throughout America as there is such a large quilting network. She also teaches at workshops organized by quilting societies. But she is happiest when she is at home and working on a new project.

# ROBIN SCHWALB

Robin Schwalb is a native New Yorker who graduated in liberal arts, with a painting major, from the State University of New York in 1974. Her first job after she graduated was as a hand weaver for a large fabric company and it was here that she met another weaver who introduced her to quilting. She felt completely at home with quilts and has said that 'cloth is a tactile and sensual delight'. She was soon inspired to try her hand at making 'contained-crazy' quilts. These quilts were all machine pieced and in turn led her to incorporate language and writing in her work.

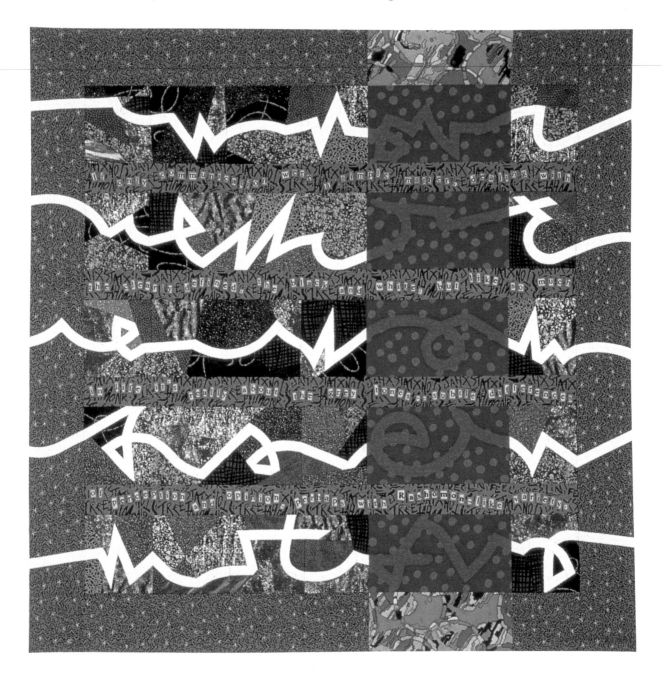

*Above:* Here, stencilled cottons have been machine pieced, hand appliquéd and then quilted.

*Left:* Cottons and cotton blend appliqué work are combined here with overdyed
and machine pieced appliqué and hand quilting.

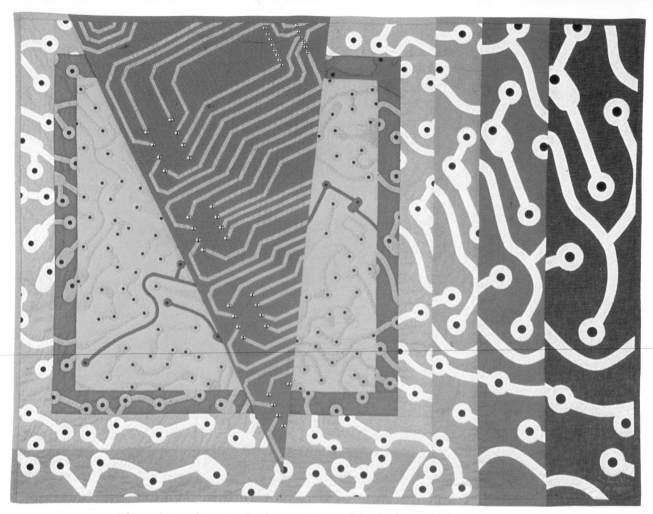

This work is machine pieced with cotton fabrics and the details are added with metal studs.
It is then partly hand appliquéd, partly quilted.

Many of Robin's quilts and fabric collages explore 'the rich variety of the written word'. She uses written symbols and words in her work, but disguises them in various ways – in obsolete languages or concealing the text within the quilting – because she does not want the tendency to read the text to disrupt the intuitive responses to her work. This exploration of language and writing led Robin to employ a number of different techniques, including silk screen printing, stencilling, dyeing, piecing, quilting and appliqué. Appliqué is used particularly when a more fluid and organic design is required. One of her early appliqué quilts won the 1989 Quilt National Award of Excellence. Nowadays Robin uses a combination of various techniques and hand or machine stitches the motifs in place depending upon their shape.

Robin's inspirations come largely with her job –
she is a projectionist at the Metropolitan Museum of Art in New York. In addition, there are the tiny details that people take for granted: circuit boards are an especial favourite, and the millions of things to see in the busy streets of New York City.

She tries to translate her inspirations into sketches but they often turn out as vague scribbles. However, once the main core of the piece is designed, Robin starts work directly with the fabric; she makes no mock-up.

Her work is not really marketed as such, partly because of the time it takes her to make appliquéd pieces and partly because she has a full time job. Nevertheless, she has sold a few pieces personally or through a friend acting as a corporate consultant. Her job restricts her free time and so she does not teach, although she has lectured in the past.

# HAYLEY SMITH

Hayley Smith is an artist who works exclusively in stumpwork. She makes wonderful detailed three-dimensional pictures from fabric and thread. Artistry runs in the family for both her parents are craft-workers: her mother works mainly in textiles and her father makes cabinets. However, Hayley is the first in her family to attend art school, graduating in carpet design at Kidderminster College of Art.

A tribute to a rather famous husband and wife television presenting team. The detailing is given special attention since the pieces are so small.

This wonderful work uses heavily machine embroidered fabric with glittery thread which is then appliquéd onto the background. *Trapunto*, when the piece is stuffed from behind once it has been sewn down, is used to pad out the figure, and embroidery stitches and scraps of fabric as well as coloured pencils give the finishing details.

When one sees the delicacy of Hayley's work it is hard to believe she did carpet design. She was making tufted rugs with knitted borders when she left college. She took her work to Gabhani O'Keefe, the interior designer, who suggested she put some stumpwork on them. Hayley taught herself how and has never looked back.

Quotes from fairy stories, songs, lines from poems and children's poetry books are all influences. Occasionally she is commissioned to make a piece of work based on a poem. In fact, a recent commission was from a man living in an Arts and Crafts house who wanted a piece from 'Goblin Market' by Christina Rossetti. American folk art and the way the flat primitive figures look directly at the viewer also motivates Hayley.

Most of her designs come directly from her own imagination and go straight onto the calico. Unlike most of the other artists and designers in this book, she does not keep a sketchbook. Instead, she quickly sketches out an idea and then immediately paints it. She prefers to work colour in the form of thread in preference to paint. Embroidery silks and machine embroidery threads are her key materials. She stretches calico across an embroidery frame and then applies a machine embroidered background on top of which she does stumpwork.

Hayley sells her work through trade fairs, small craft shops, exhibitions, private commissions, the

This pleasantly plump character is almost lifelike. Her skirt is made of netting which is attached at the waist and sticks out like a tutu.

Suffolk Craft Society and the Essex Craft Society, of whom she is a founder member.

She teaches some local and residential courses and gives workshops in the Bristol and Bath area. As well as practical courses, Hayley also gives lectures on the history of stumpwork.

*See pages 100–101 for instructions on how to make a brooch designed by Hayley Smith.*

This work is typical of the artist's wit and attention to detail. Her specialized technique is stumpwork, creating padded figurative work from appliqué and then embroidering over that.

# LISA VAUGHAN

Lisa Vaughan started her design training by taking an HND in print at Derby College of Art, although it was with a sewing machine that she found she could get effects she preferred – witness the cushions, blankets, bed and table linen, aprons, handkerchiefs and bags she makes today. After leaving college she produced embroideries which were translated into print designs but after a year she began to get bored and thought her techniques were not progressing. She decided instead to apply to the Royal College of Art and got a place to study embroidery.

During the first year, her work changed completely. One of her first year projects was to produce an embroidered and appliquéd design measuring 25 x 12.5cm (10 x 5in) which was then chosen to be made into a rug in Turkey. This took a year and the finished rug measured 2.4 x 1.5m (8 x 5ft).

Later, Lisa went to India on a work placement for a company who made block prints and weaves for interiors and fashions. Before her trip, she had wanted to produce fabric pictures; her India experience made her want to produce practical items. When she returned to Britain, she started working on her degree show, developing ideas for bed linen and

*Above:* A fresh and lively pillowcase, typical of the artist, has quirky figures and colours and can only bring good cheer.

*Right:* The front cushion is called *She found a chequered heart* and is a natural coloured blanket with blanket stitching around the edges and a tartan heart motif. The cushion in the background is called *Squeeze me*, very apt and very refreshing.

A selection of blankets with different appliqué methods and details.

blankets. She had a very good response to her degree show: Designers' Guild asked her to do some work and she did some illustrations for *Vogue*. She was also awarded a Crafts Council grant. In 1993 she was chosen for the Chelsea Crafts Fair where she acquired more new clients. She sells her work in Japan and America; she has designed for Habitat.

She is always collecting things, going to exhibitions and leafing through books. She keeps a sketchbook which is full of drawings and designs, words and phrases. The bits of writing are split up and put together in different ways. Another way she has of building up compositions is to make montages from photographs, sometimes using the whole montage, other times just taking elements out of it.

The materials Lisa uses depend upon the work and whether it is commissioned. She likes cottons, linens, wools, velvet, mohair and silk. Her blankets are made out of new blankets which are cut up and pieced together and then have appliquéd motifs applied to them. The blanket stitch around the edges is done by hand which makes it very time consuming and therefore expensive.

Lisa teaches multimedia weave and print design at Loughborough College of Art.

*See pages 112–113 and 114–115 for instructions on how to make a panelled blanket and a pillowcase designed by Lisa Vaughan.*

# KIRSTEN WATTS

Kirsten was taught appliqué by her mother when she was a child. This early experience inspired her to study printmaking and textiles for 'A' levels and to go on to Middlesex University to do a degree in printed textiles.

Her work allows her to undertake projects that demand the quality of hand sewing together with the use of print and a variety of textures. She particularly likes fake fur for its texture. She uses simply cut motifs from blankets, woollens, fake furs and lamés to achieve a variety of textures and a naïve feel to the overall look of the finished piece.

Kirsten declares that her influences derive from the multiplicity of genres and circumstance that are apparent in contemporary British lifestyles. In particular, she observes the idiosyncrasies in people going about their various activities, ranging from walking to sunbathing. Her earlier work was extremely simple, using basic shapes and forms reminiscent of cave paintings, which were mainly cream and black. However, she has moved on to incorporate several images in one piece and a shock of different colours.

She takes photographs to capture features from everyday life and then works on them in a sketchbook. She then scales up her designs to their final size before beginning work on the fabrics. Apart from appliqué a lot of her work is screen printed before being cut into motifs for appliqué. Her best known work is perhaps her greetings cards which feature her idiosyncratic and amusing figures and animals.

She sells her work in a couple of shops in London and in Camden Market during the summer and exhibits at a number of craft shows.

*See pages 122–123 for instructions on how to make a picture blanket designed by Kirsten Watts.*

This *Picture blanket*, which quotes '*It's a dog's life*', uses a variety of unusual fabrics for the appliqué – fake fur and plastic – but is also screen printed.

# TECHNIQUES

✳

Before you start

Basic hand-stitched appliqué

Bonding

Stumpwork

Shadow appliqué

Reverse appliqué

Machine appliqué

Inlay work

## BEFORE YOU START

Appliqué is a craft that requires no special and expensive tools – a needle, some thread and various bits and pieces of fabric as well as the tools found in most sewing boxes will be more than sufficient for your purposes.

Below are more precise details about these standard tools and some information about the basic techniques it is best to know before getting started on any projects.

### Tools and Materials

#### Needles and thimbles

You will need a selection of needles in various sizes for the different thicknesses of fabrics, yarns and threads. A thimble is good for when you are pushing a needle through thick layers of material.

#### Threads

Cotton and polyester threads are generally fine for most appliqué work. A white or black cotton thread is suitable for tacking motifs in place before sewing them down properly. Embroidery threads and silks can be used to embroider intricate details, such as the stems on flowers, facial features and any writing.

If you are going to embroider with a sewing machine, use machine embroidery thread, the strands of which are thinner than regular embroidery silk.

Crochet and knitting yarns can be used to give texture and depth.

#### Fabric

Collect a variety of fabrics – different colours, textures, patterns and thicknesses. Keep scraps that are left over from dressmaking, go to jumble sales and markets and try to acquire a substantial palette before you begin.

Any kind of material can be used for appliqué, although it is important to choose the right kind of fabric for a particular design or for the purpose for which it is being made. For example, if you are deco-

Threads are a prerequisite for this craft. A wide range is available, including embroidery threads, sewing polyesters and silky machine embroidery rayon.

rating furnishings, factors such as durability and ease of cleaning may need considering.

The fibres in wool and animal hair fabrics, such as cashmere and angora, hold air and so give elasticity and depth, as well as feeling and looking very soft. Silk can be hard to work with but its suppleness allows it to drape gracefully. It has a slight sheen which gives lustre to its rich jewel-like colours.

Cotton fabrics, of which there are many, including corduroy, poplin, lawn and voile, are good to use for either appliqué pieces or as backgrounds. They are easy to handle and dye well.

Man-made fibres like nylon, acrylic and rayon are ideal for appliquéing objects that need to be durable.

Bear in mind that some fabrics fray more than others and that non-woven materials like leather, suede and felt do not fray at all. The latter are therefore probably the easier materials to start with.

It is well worth experimenting with more unusual materials – fake furs, foils, plastics and papers – to achieve novel effects.

### Scissors

It is imperative that the scissors you use are very sharp, otherwise the motifs you cut out won't be to your exact design. Blunt scissors will pucker and pull fabric, especially fabrics that fray easily. A pair of dressmakers' scissors and a small pair of scissors are needed to cut out motifs. A pair of pinking shears give fabric an interesting cut, and this form of edging is ideal for fabrics that don't fray. Also a pair of paper scissors are useful when cutting the paper patterns and templates.

### Dressmaking pins and pin cushions

Pins are needed to position motifs onto the background material while arranging a design and to secure the motifs whilst tacking is being carried out. A pin cushion keeps them handy.

*Above:* A mélange of rich and luxurious fabrics including brocade, slub silk and metallic prints as well as more humble homespun checks, can all be used for appliqué work.

Just some of the more specific tools useful for the art of appliqué – large cutting out scissors, pinking shears and an embroidery hoop to hold material taut while embellishing it with hand or machine stitches.

Iron, sewing machine, scissors, tape measure, pens and pencils
are all useful tools for appliqué.

### Embroidery frame

A frame can be useful when you want to hold the
background fabric taut while you work on a particular section of your appliqué. It will stop the background fabric from puckering and ensure that the
applied motif lies flat.

### Sewing machine

A sewing machine with embroidery foot fixtures is
necessary for machine appliqué. Machine satin stitch
is ideal for the main sewing involved in stained glass
appliqué and the zigzag stitch is handy for securing
motifs and for decoration.

### Iron and ironing board

An iron is needed not only for the final pressing of a
finished piece, but it is extremely useful when turning
under seam allowances before tacking. If you use
interfacing or fusible webbing, an iron is necessary
to heat and press the backing onto the fabric.

### Interfacing and fusible webbing

Interfacing is used to stiffen and give structure to
flimsy materials. In appliqué it is very useful for
backing awkward shapes, so enabling the seam
allowance to be folded back onto the interfacing and
thus give a definite outline.

Fusible webbing is double sided and can be used
to structure appliqué motifs. The backing paper can
be peeled off and the same side can be ironed into
position onto the background material. This saves
having to tack the design in place.

### Sketchbook, paper, card, pencils and pens

These artists' materials are optional but are a great
help for working out designs prior to creating the
appliqué itself. They are basically used to formulate
ideas and keep a record of designs. You can also
cull ideas from magazines – for example, cut out
any photographs you like and place them by your
sketches, then work with the two against each other,
letting them inspire you and think of new ideas.

The card is for any templates you decide to make.

### Dressmakers' carbon, tracing and graph paper

Dressmakers' carbon paper is used to transfer the
design onto heavier and darker material. Tracing
paper can be used either to trace the design onto a
light coloured fabric or to make paper templates for
the appliqué motifs. Graph paper is for scaling up
designs when transferring them from your original
design into a practical pattern.

### Extras you may need

Latex glue
Sharp craft knife and cutting board
Glue stick
Ruler and set square

## Basic Techniques

Careful preparation before you actually start working on the appliqué piece should ensure good results. There are things which need to be done prior to cutting and sewing to make the process simpler and easier. If you are an experienced seamstress, you will notice that many of these basic techniques boil down to common sense. You should know before you begin what kind of appliqué you want to carry out as each appliqué technique has its own characteristics and it is necessary to use the right methods for cutting and applying the motifs.

### Preparing fabrics

Check whether or not your fabrics are colourfast and pre-shrunk. If not, wash them before you begin to avoid the possibility of washing the finished item and finding that it puckers and becomes patchy. Make sure that the fabrics are clean and pressed flat. Also check that the grain of the fabric is straight. You can do this by pulling out a weft thread near one end and cutting along it.

Certain techniques need a backing fabric. This is not the same as a background fabric – it is the fabric behind the background and acts as a support for the appliqué but it is not visible as it is completely covered in appliqué. Some lightweight fabrics require a backing fabric to add strength and extra weight, especially for wall-hangings and panels. Cotton-type fabrics are ideal for backing; cotton lawn is a good backing for fine fabrics; calico is good for heavier materials. Ensure that it is pre-washed and that it is at least 10cm (4in) larger than the background fabric to allow for seam allowances.

### Scaling up the design

When you have decided on a design, scale it up to the size you want to work at. To do this, draw a grid over your original design, then copy it square by square onto a larger grid. Alternatively, enlarge it to the required size on a photocopier.

### Transferring the design

If the fabric you plan to work on is of a light colour, you will be able to trace the design directly onto it using tailor's chalk or a non-permanent pen. If the fabric is thick or dark, use dressmakers' carbon paper. Don't use office carbon as this will leave permanent marks.

### Preparing paper templates

Appliqué pieces generally correspond to areas of the original design and if you are using dressmakers' carbon, you will be able to trace the patterns directly onto your appliqué fabric. Otherwise, you should make a paper pattern of the design and then cut this into corresponding appliqué templates for you to draw around on to the appliqué fabric. If the design is quite complex, mark off each individual piece with a number and mark its place on the background fabric with the same number.

Embroidery perlé threads, buttonhole thread and tassels made from pinked trimmings in brightly dyed colours are threaded and knotted together through a cotton reel.

### Cutting out appliqué motifs

Work on a flat surface when cutting out your appliqué motifs so that the fabric does not draw or pucker. Use very sharp dressmakers' scissors to ensure an exact replica of the original design; blunt scissors never cut as well as you would like them to. Remember to leave appropriate seam allowances for fabrics which fray and need turning under. Before positioning pieces with a seam allowance, unless you are working on very intricate pieces, turn under the seam allowance, press and then tack. Non-woven fabrics do not need an allowance.

### Using backing pieces

Iron-on interfacing and fusible webbing are designed to support fabrics. When used on appliqué pieces, especially those with an unusual shape, they give definition, help disguise turned under edges and give substance to flimsier fabrics. For machine appliqué, the interfacing should be ironed on, the motif cut out and then zigzag stitched onto the background material without a turning.

Iron-on interfacing is available in a variety of different qualities depending on the type of fabric. To use iron-on interfacing, draw around the paper template onto the shiny, adhesive side of the interfacing with a pencil. Cut out the shape and iron it, shiny side down, onto the wrong side of the material. Then cut around the interfacing and material, leaving a small seam allowance, and fold the seam allowance over the interfacing. Press and tack. It is now ready to apply to the background material.

Fusible webbing is adhesive on both sides. This means that it is not necessary to tack the motif onto the background prior to the main sewing. It is suitable for materials that fray and is particularly appropriate for stained glass appliqué.

It is applied in a similar way to the iron-on interfacing. Place the webbing on a flat surface with the smooth side (the non-adhesive side) facing up. Lay the template the wrong side up onto the webbing and draw around it. Cut out the webbing, leaving an allowance all the way around the shape. Lay this with the rough (adhesive) side down onto the wrong side of the material and press. When it has cooled, cut along the exact outline then peel off the backing paper. Position onto the background material and iron into position.

### Working on corners

When you are sewing down a square or rectangular appliqué motif and you approach a corner, sew almost to the end of the side that you are on. Just before you reach the end, turn under the adjacent side and stitch it down at a 45 degree angle. Turn in the side that you have already sewn, turn under and stitch that down. Continue on to the other side. This process is also called mitring.

### Working on curves and circles

Before you even begin to sew a circular or rounded piece, snip around the whole edge on the seam allowance. When you fold it under, the fabric will give slightly and will prevent corners from forming.

### Making bias binding or crossway strips

Crossway strips can be used in stained glass appliqué as well as for binding the edges of work. If you make your own strips, you are guaranteed that they will match what you are working on; shop-bought strips are available only in a small range of colours.

Fold a square of fabric into a triangle and then mark off parallel lines to the diagonal fold at 2.5cm (1in) intervals. Cut the marked fabric carefully into strips, sew these strips together on the straight grain of the fabric to make one length and then fold under the raw edges and press firmly.

To make a rouleaux strip, work in the same manner as for the crossway strip but sew the long raw edges together and turn inside out before you press.

## BASIC HAND-STITCHED APPLIQUÉ

The easiest fabrics to use for hand-stitched appliqué, in fact for any appliqué, are those that do not fray. Among these are felt, suede, leather and interfacing – basically, materials that are non-woven and not prone to unravelling. If a material is non-woven, then it is less likely to stretch or distort and, of course, there is no need to turn under the edges. Such fabrics can also be attached to the background fabric with

bonding (see page 83) which is a huge time saving device. However, for appliqué it is not always the best option to choose the easiest of fabrics to work with, for the massive array of different materials and fabrics gives almost unlimited scope.

The basic tools you will need to do a simple appliqué job are: two contrasting fabrics; sharp scissors; interfacing (to give crisp edges to awkward shapes); needle and thread; paper and pencil.

Indian appliqué cushion cover made traditionally by tacking and then hand sewing each piece.

Basic hand-stitched appliqué, traditionally the most popular method, is used here. Pieces of material are tacked into position, and the edges are turned under and sewn with tiny overstitches.

1 Firstly, decide on your motif and draw it on paper. If necessary, use it as a template by cutting it out and drawing around it onto the right side of your chosen appliqué fabric.

2 Cut around the motif, making sure you handle the fabric carefully. If it is a fabric that frays, leave a seam allowance of approximately 0.5cm (1/4 in) for turning under.

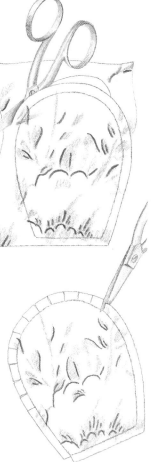

3 If you leave a seam allowance there is an extra step if the motif has curved edges. Clip the curved edges at right angles to the actual motif line and to the edge of that line. Straight edges do not need to be clipped.

4 If you wish, you can turn over, press and tack the raw edges of the motif before you sew it onto the background. If you want a crisp edge to an unusual or curved shape, cut interfacing to the exact size of

the motif (without a seam allowance). Place this centrally on the wrong side of the motif and tack it down, turning the raw edges over onto the interfacing.

5 Pin or tack your motif onto the background with the right side facing up. For curved or difficult areas, push the seam allowances under with the tip of your needle as you sew and smooth them over with your finger. Use slip stitch. Remove all tacking stitches.

*For projects using this technique, see the following:*
Chequered waistcoat (pages 96–97)
Cacti cacophony wash bag (pages 98–99)
Blue silk book (pages 108–109)
All-seeing hands scarf (pages 110–111)
Floating leaves and bunting blanket (pages 112–113)
Airmail pillowcase (pages 114–115)
Gingham fish cushion (pages 120–121)
Picture blanket (pages 122–123)

## BONDING, OR FUSED APPLIQUÉ

Bonding fabrics with interfacing or fusible webbing can be an alternative to sewing. This is especially good for items that are either small and difficult to stitch or ones that are not in constant use. It is ideal for intricate outlines on flimsy material as it adds structure and stiffness, and stops it from stretching.

You can also use this technique as an alternative to turning under a seam allowance as it prevents the fabric from fraying.

Light coloured and white fabrics, when applied onto a dark background material, can look transparent and hem turnings can show through. These problems can be remedied by fusing the light coloured fabric with another layer of material or bonding it onto interfacing.

However, bonding fabrics with interfacing or webbing is generally used as a preparation to sewing and not purely as its own method.

Bonding is a traditional appliqué technique; starches and pastes were used before today's modern equivalents.

*For projects using this technique,*
*see the following:*
Cacti cacophony wash bag (pages 98–99)
Starry lampshade (pages 106–107)
Blue silk book (pages 108–109)
Jamboree buttons (pages 116–117)
Pop Art bag (pages 118–119)
Gingham fish cushion (pages 120–121)
Picture blanket (pages 122–123)

For bonded appliqué, the fabrics are ironed together with fusible webbing and then embellished.

## STUMPWORK

Stumpwork is a method of creating a three-dimensional effect by using detached stitching and padding shapes either before or after applying them to the base material. Detached buttonhole and needle lace stitches, as well as embossed embroidery, were very popular in Elizabethan times, especially for ecclesiastical cloths and banners. The techniques combined through time and became known as stumpwork (although this was not the name used until Victorian times, and there seems to be no record of the origins of the name).

It was an extremely favoured technique throughout the reign of Charles I, when embroidery was a very fashionable pastime for ladies of the court. The earliest evidence for this dates back to 1640. For some reason, however, this popularity lasted only about 40 years and stumpwork then almost disappeared, to re-emerge as a fashion again only in Victorian times.

The applied motifs or, as they were called in Elizabethan times, 'slips' because the designs were often taken from slips or cuttings of plants and flowers, were cut from fine canvas or linen and then applied to silk or velvet. They were worked in detached buttonhole stitch, which raised them in relief from the background. The technique was used for decorating frames, caskets and for creating narrative pictures.

Although the results are generally the same, there are several different ways in which to achieve this three-dimensional effect with your applied pieces. The first technique is to pad the appliqué motifs from the front once they are partially attached to the background fabric:

1 Use the procedure for basic hand-stitched appliqué (see pages 81-82).

2 Leave a small opening when you are slip stitching the applied shape onto the base material.

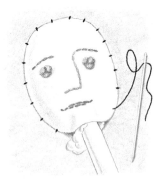

3 Insert stuffing, either wadding or cotton wool, and use a crochet hook or a knitting needle to work the stuffing gently into the corners and to pad the motif as you wish.

Stumpwork, a form of raised embroidery, reached its peak of popularity in the mid-seventeenth century. It is a slow and methodical method of appliqué and here the fabric is made up of rows of buttonhole stitch, known as corded filling.

4 Close up the opening carefully, ensuring that the stitches are close enough together so that the stuffing cannot escape.

The alternative and most popular method is *trapunto*. This is when the work is stuffed from the rear once the appliquéd piece is sewn down:

1  Sew the appliqué piece onto the background, making sure that the stitches come through to the reverse of the work so that you can see the outline when you start working from the back.

2  Turn the work over so that the wrong side is facing up and, with a sharp craft knife or scissors, cut a small slit into the centre back of the appliquéd piece.

3  Stuff small pieces of wadding into the opening using a cro-chet hook or a large needle, being careful not to tear the slit open any further.

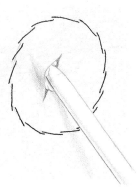

4  Once the shape is stuffed to your liking, close up the slit using close overstitch, making sure that the stuffing cannot escape in between the stitches.

Graduated padding, which is smooth and rounded, can be achieved with several fabric shapes, each cut smaller than the other and then placed in a layered stack. The appliqué shape is then placed over this and the raw edges are turned under and sewn down with slip stitch.

Yet another way to create a three-dimensional effect is to make padded shapes first and then just sew them onto the background. You need to cut two identical appliqué pieces, sew them together with the right sides facing, turn them the right way round, stuff them with wadding through a small opening, close the opening and then sew the whole thing onto the background. Although this method is time consuming, the effect is well worth the time as the piece stands out very much in relief to the other types of padding. It really is the ideal way of making one piece stand out from the others in your work.

***For projects using this technique, see the following:***
Funny face brooch (pages 100–101)
Velvet jester hat (pages 102–103)
Fabric flower brooch (pages 104–105)

## SHADOW APPLIQUÉ

The shadow appliqué technique uses transparent fabric to give a shadowy effect to applied pieces of fabric. The basic method is to appliqué plain fabric shapes onto a background material and cover these shapes with a sheer fabric which is then sewn in place. You can either trim around the appliquéd shape to make it stand out or sew down the transparent fabric along the outside border of the whole piece to give an almost quilted result.

Any material which is lightweight and transparent is suitable: organdie; chiffon; voile; georgette; organza and netting. By playing with colours and materials you can achieve subtle effects: if you lay white organza over red material, it can appear pink; if you place yellow voile over blue applied fabric it can look green.

1  Draw your design on paper and transfer it, using carbon paper, to the right side of the background fabric.

2  Use the same paper pattern to create templates for the appliqué pieces. Draw around the template onto the fabric (there is no need to add a seam allowance). Cut out the shapes with a very sharp pair of scissors, trying to prevent the fabric from fraying.

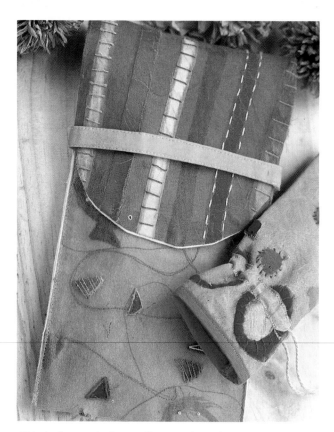

This shadow-worked purse illustrates the technique of appliquéing plain fabric shapes onto a background, then covering them in sheer fabric to reveal the shapes below.

3 Glue the shapes into position on the marked background fabric.

4 Place a sheet of transparent material, the size of the background, over the entire work, sandwiching the applied pieces in between the background and the top layer. Tack all around the outer edges of the fabrics, securing them together. Also tack around the actual appliqué design.

5 With a contrasting thread or embroidery silk, sew around the appliqué pieces using tiny running, satin or buttonhole stitch. The sewing should be exactly on the edge of the appliqué or directly next to it.

6 Remove the tacking if you want to trim around the appliqué so that only the motif is shadowed. Alternatively, leave the tacking intact while you sew around the outer edges of the whole piece to introduce an almost quilted effect to the work.

*For projects using this technique, see the following:*
Fabric flower brooch (pages 104–105)

### REVERSE APPLIQUÉ

This technique is called reverse appliqué because it is the opposite method of traditional appliqué – you are removing fabric shapes rather than adding them. It is also known as multi-layered appliqué. Several layers of fabric are tacked together, all with their right sides facing up, and the layers are then cut back in patterns to reveal the different colours and fabrics beneath. Everything is then sewn into place.

This method has been worked for centuries by the Kuna Indian women in Panama's San Blas Islands. Traditionally, the work is made into panels of yoked, short-sleeved blouses called *molas*. Using several layers of different coloured vivid fabrics, patterns are cut away, through one or two or many of the layers, to reveal these colours. The designs are reminiscent of their ancestors' body paintings, which are translated into the intricate reverse appliqué technique, portraying asymmetrical patterns showing figures of people, animals and demons.

A fine example of reverse appliqué using soft and transparent fabric layered over rich silk. The top layer has been cut away to reveal the fabric beneath. The cut work has then been sewn around the edges to secure the fabric in position.

Reverse appliqué is also a traditional craft in Southeast Asia where the *pa nau* is the needlework tradition of the Hmong cultures in Vietnam and Thailand. It is visible on many everyday objects from hats and bags to bedspreads. Although the method is the same as that of the Kuna Indians, the designs and styles are very different indeed. The Hmong designs are of simple animal outlines or geometric patterns and embroidery is used to add highlight and detail to the work.

The basic technique, like all appliqué techniques, is relatively simple:

1  Draw your motif on paper and mark it off onto the right side of the fabric that you would like to be at the top. Place the other fabrics in layers

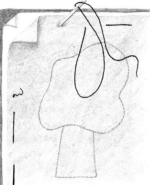

beneath this, all facing the right way up. Tack around the edges going through all the layers.

2  Tack around the outside of your motif, leaving a small border. Go through all the layers. Using a small and very sharp pair of scissors, cut through the top layer within the marked line. Be careful not to cut through the second layer.

3  Clip around the edges of the cut work up to the edge of the actual motif. This will help ease the raw edge under into a hem. Turn under the hem with your needle as you go along and, using a thread that

matches the top fabric, slip stitch the top layer down onto the second layer.

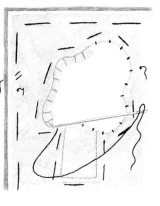

4 If you want to work on into the next layer, ensure that you have firmly stitched the first and second layer together.

5 Repeat steps one and two onto the second layer of fabric, then cut through the second layer to reveal the third. Slip stitch the second and third layers of fabric together.

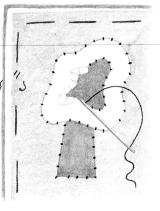

A variation on this technique is the patchwork reverse appliqué, where different coloured patches are applied to the backing fabric. The top layer is then cut through in random patterns to allow the coloured patchwork to show through.

The best types of fabrics used for this kind of appliqué are lightweight cottons. Fabrics that fray should be avoided because of the intricate cutting involved. Heavy fabrics should be avoided too, as they become bulky when they are cut and turned under. Remember that the bottom layer acts as the lining and the backing, so it should never be cut through.

***For projects using this technique, see the following:***
Starry lampshade (pages 106–107)
Blue silk book (pages 108–109)

## MACHINE APPLIQUÉ

Having a sewing machine is a definite advantage when you appliqué, not only for speed, but also for the strength and variety of the stitches. Sewing machine stitches are very hard wearing and are ideal for decorating hard wearing things such as bags, bedding, most household articles and children's clothes. Under hard wear, hand stitching does not really hold up to the strength of machine stitching. Machine satin stitch is much bolder and less time consuming than hand satin stitch and is ideal as a sharp outline to your applied motif or for filling in areas with stitches.

When using a sewing machine for appliqué, attach the appliqué foot. This has a wide gap between the prongs and a groove on the underside. If you do not have an appliqué foot, use the zigzag foot instead.

1 If the fabric is thin or flimsy you may want to give it stability by ironing interfacing onto the wrong side of the fabric. Draw your motifs onto the right side of the fabric and cut them out.

2 Arrange the appliqué motifs into the correct positions on the background fabric. You can secure them by a variety of methods: tacking; glue or fusible webbing.

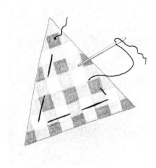

3 Thread the sewing machine with a matching cotton thread and sew the applied motifs down. Stitch close to the edges with the machine set on either an open zigzag stitch or a

medium straight stitch. Do this carefully to avoid puckering.

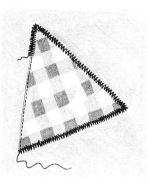

4 Set the sewing machine onto a close zigzag satin stitch and sew along the edges of the applied pieces, covering both the previous stitches and the raw edge. Leave a long thread end when you begin.

5 Guide the fabric around, without piling the stitches up or leaving gaps. When working on corners, sew up to the corner, leave the needle in the fabric, lift the foot, turn the fabric in the right direction, drop the foot and carry on sewing.

6 To finish off, leave another long thread end. Pull the threads from the beginning and the end through to the wrong side of the fabric and sew them into the back of the work.

*Another method is invisible machine appliqué:*

1 Cut out the motifs, adding a small seam allowance around each one. Cut interfacing to the exact measurements of the motif, without a seam allowance. Iron the interfacing onto the wrong side of the motif to fuse it in place.

Detail of a lampshade (see page 106), worked in reverse appliqué, where the top layer is cut away to reveal the layer below.

2  Fold the seam allowance under onto the wrong side and tack it down. Then tack the motif onto the background.

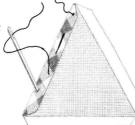

3  Set the machine onto small straight stitch. With the inner right edge of the foot on the folded edge, sew along the edge. The needle should catch the very edge of the motif.

*For projects using this technique, see the following:*

Cards are a wise choice for machine-stitch appliqué – it is a quick method and so can be used to produce more than one of an item.

## INLAY WORK

Inlay appliqué is a variation on basic hand-stitched appliqué technique, the difference being that with inlay work, the applied piece is sewn *into* a background and with the basic method, the applied piece is sewn *onto* the background.

In the nineteenth century, inlay work was referred to as mosaic work since the fabric pieces slotted together like a mosaic or a jigsaw. Felt is the ideal material to use because it does not fray and could be stitched invisibly, so creating a smooth and flat piece of work.

This is a simple method and is good for making big and bold projects, such as banners and wall-hangings. In the late nineteenth and early twentieth centuries, it was popular in ecclesiastical embroideries, adorning banners and altar cloths made from heavy velvets and brocades. Gold cord or piping generally covered or 'couched' the joins between the motif and background.

1  Place one non-fraying fabric underneath another of a contrasting colour, both with the right sides facing up. Pin them onto a cutting mat and draw your design on the right side of the top fabric.

2  When you are satisfied with your drawing, cut through both pieces using a sharp craft knife. Do this carefully and accurately, as both the materials need to be cut identically.

3  Remove both the motifs that you have cut out of the material to reveal the outline.

This Adam and Eve scene was made using inlay pieces sewn *into* rather than *onto* the background material, so that they become one with it.

4  Tack one of the backgrounds onto a piece of base material – interfacing or a lightweight material. Insert the contrasting coloured motif into the background, easing it into place. It should fit perfectly. Pin or tack it in place.

5  For a quick result you can glue both the pieces onto the base material. Otherwise you can choose from a selection of embroidery stitches to sew the edges together, going over the cut edges of the background and the motif.

A prowling Bengal tiger is an example of how striking the method of inlay work can look.

6  Once the shapes are in position the joins can be neatened by adding braiding, cord or piping as an alternative to embroidery stitches.

7  If the base material is a good strong fabric, you can turn under the cut edges of the inlaid areas and hem them down, creating a channel of a third colour in between the motif and background.

**Reverse inlay**

When you cut out a motif from one fabric and a background from another to do inlay appliqué, you are left with two motifs and two backgrounds – for example, one black and the other white. This means that you can make contrasting designs by placing the white motif in the black 'frame' and the black motif in the white 'frame'. You can then place 'both' framed motifs alongside each other to create a reverse inlay effect.

Accuracy in cutting out the motifs is of the utmost importance for this technique, otherwise the motifs just will not fit into the frame.

## Machine inlay

This is also known as *découpé* and is an even quicker way of inlaying appliqué with a sewing machine.

1 Tack two contrasting fabrics together with the right sides facing up. Mark off your design on the top fabric and sew around it on the right side of the top layer.

2 Take a very sharp pair of small scissors and cut out the top layer, from the inside of the machine stitched line, leaving a minimal border.

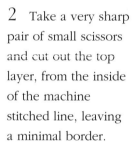

3 Remove the tacking stitches and then sew over the machine stitch and border with a satin stitch on your machine.

4 Turn the piece the wrong way round and then trim away the excess fabric of the bottom layer.

## Applied inlay

This is yet another variation on the inlay technique. Again it is a simple procedure but the result adds dimension to any kind of appliqué.

1 Work a design in your chosen appliqué method. Using the same templates, cut the same number of shapes in contrasting colours for the inlay pieces. There is no need to make seam allowances. Clip the corners of the inlays to make turning them under easier.

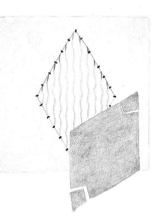

2 Place the inlay pieces over their partner appliquéd shapes and tack them into position.

3 Once they are secure, slip stitch each piece down, turning the raw edges under as you go along. Try to keep the same width between the edges of the inlay and those of the appliqué so that the channels are even.

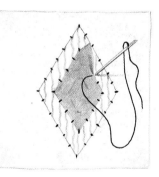

*For projects using this technique, see the following:*
Ethnic by design bag (pages 124–125)

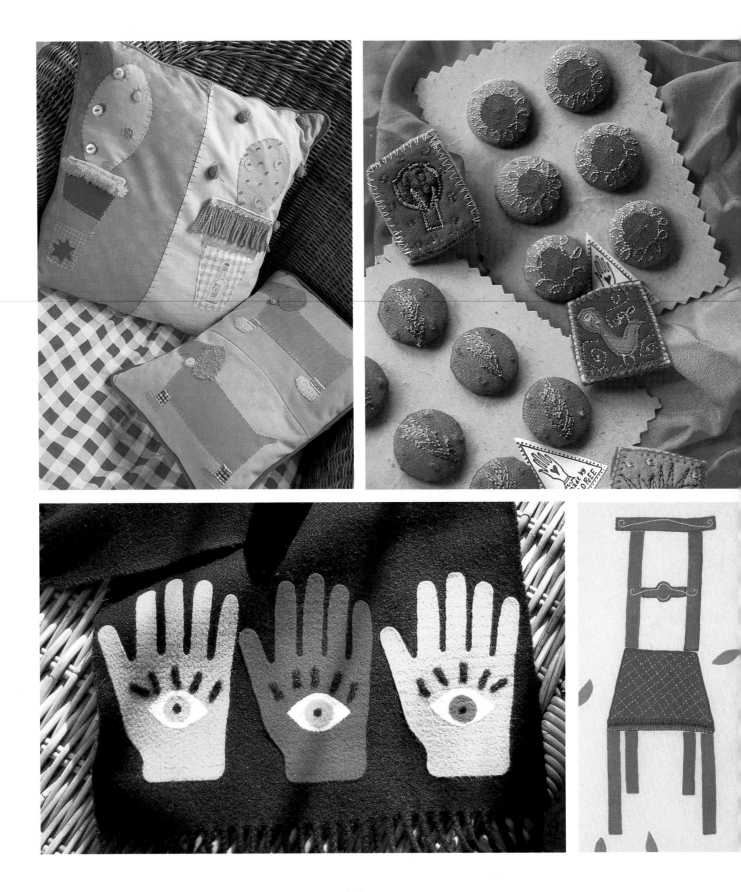

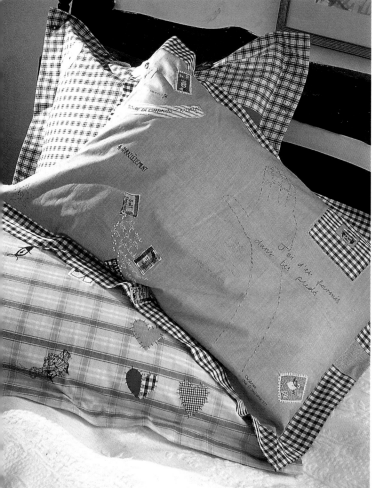

# PROJECTS

✳

# CHEQUERED WAISTCOAT

## MADELAINE MILLINGTON

*Techniques used: basic hand-stitched appliqué (see pages 81-82)*

1 Following the maker's instructions, dye half the fabric and piping cord red and the other half yellow. Using the fabric paint and sponge, stamp red squares on three-quarters of the yellow fabric. Iron the back of the fabric in order to fix the paint.

2 Cut out the pattern pieces, using the stamped fabric for the lining and the plain red and yellow fabric for the rest of the waistcoat. Make your own pattern for the tails, cutting two pieces of fabric that will fit along the back waist seam and two identical lining pieces.

3 Attach the tails to the back bodice before making up the waistcoat. With right sides facing, place the tail piece and its lining together, sew around the edges, leaving a 1.5cm (5/8in) seam allowance and leave the top open. Turn it the right way round and place the top open edges against the waistline of the back bodice piece. With right sides together, sew along this line. Leave one edge of the lined tail piece unsewn.

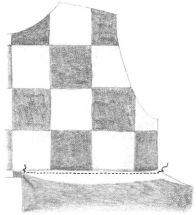

4 Press the open edge under and close it onto the waist seam with slip stitch. Top stitch around the edge of the tail piece in a running stitch, using a coloured embroidery thread.

*Left:* This detail of the waistcoat shows
that the appliqué cross is merely two
rectangles crossed over and sewn down.
The seams have been double top
stitched in contrasting colours.

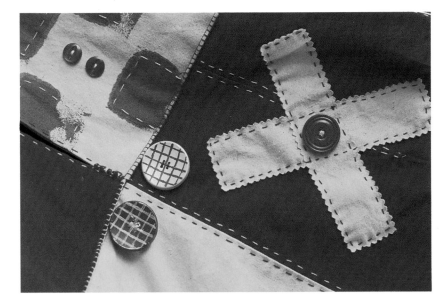

5 Sew the outside of the waistcoat according to the pattern, alternating red and yellow panels.

6 Sew over all the seams, using blanket stitch around the waist seam and running stitch for all the others.

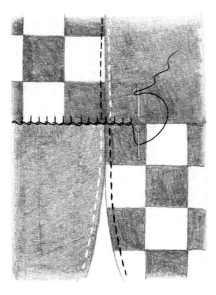

7 Decorate with buttons and buckles. Cut out stars and oblongs and sew these onto the waistcoat. You can use two oblongs to make a cross. Go over the details in running stitch using a contrasting coloured thread. Sew tassels on the end of tails.

*Right:* A traditional paper pattern was used to make this colourful waistcoat, then a tail was added. Bright appliqué motifs have been sewn on randomly. Hand stitching and couching have added even more detail to achieve that wild look.

# CACTI CACOPHONY WASH BAG
## PETRA BOASE

*Techniques used: basic hand-stitched appliqué, bonding (see pages 81–82 and 83)*

❋ YOU WILL NEED ❋
*Paper, pencil and card*
*18 x 12cm (7 1/2 x 5in) calico*
*   for the panel*
*Fabric scraps of your choice*
*Fabric for the bag, enough to*
*   accommodate the panel*
*Needle and embroidery thread*
*Fusible webbing*
*Cord*
*Safety pin*
*Buttons and beads for*
*   embellishing*

1   To make the bag, draw your design, trace it and transfer it onto card to make a template.

2   Iron the fabric scraps onto the webbing. Pin the templates onto the fabric scraps and cut out.

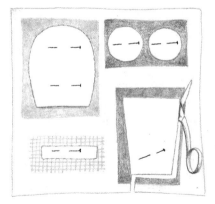

3   Peel the backing paper off the webbing and place the shapes on the main fabric. Secure them in position with a hot iron.

4   Sew or stick on patterned tape as further decoration.

5   With brightly coloured cotton, decorate the design with French knots, crosses and stab stitches. The stitches can be quite large if they are part of a naïve design.

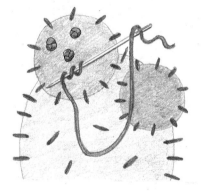

6   Fold under 5mm (1/4 in) of the edge of the panel to neaten it. Press flat.

7   To make the bag, cut the fabric into two equal rectangles.

8   Hand sew the appliqué panel onto one piece of the fabric near the bottom. With right sides facing, pin the two pieces of fabric together and seam down the

sides, leaving one short side open. Press flat.

9   On each side at the top, turn under 5cm (2in) of raw edge and machine in place.

10   Turn the top edge under 4–5 cm (1 1/2 –2in) and machine in place. Leave a small opening on one side. Thread the cord onto a safety pin and push through the opening. Undo the pin and knot the ends of the cord together.

*Above:* These colourful and cartoon-like cushion covers are simple and stunning with wonderful colour combinations and naïve stitching. The motifs are well loved and have been revamped into modern emblems.

Exuberant wash bag with cacti design, worked in bright colours and embellished with sequins.

# FUNNY FACE BROOCH

## HAYLEY SMITH

**Techniques used: stumpwork (see page 84-85)**

1   Draw a square measuring 4cm (1¹/₂ in) onto the white felt. Draw a heart in one corner. Using a sewing machine without a pressure foot, machine embroider in zigzag stitch the background using green metallic thread, and a heart using red.

2   By hand, stitch on a pink felt triangle for the neck and an oval

for the head, which should overlap the neck slightly. Leave a small opening on the head for inserting the wadding.

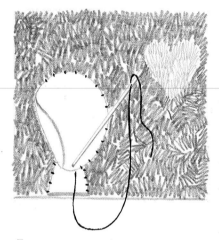

3   Add the wadding from the top and stitch round to close the opening.

4   Using thick crochet thread, sew on the hair. To make the buns, sew French knots; to make ringlets, sew bullion knots, a long thin version of French knots.

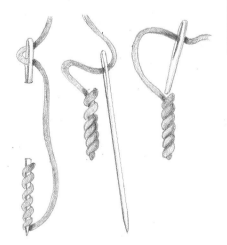

This stumpwork *Funny face brooch* is a glistening token that can be a gift for a loved one. For a perfect Valentine's present, make the portrait a personal image.

5   Using black cotton, back stitch the outline of the nose and the eyebrows. Make French knots for

the eyes and back stitch a red
cotton mouth.

6  Colour in the cheeks with
the red crayon so that there is a
suggestion of colour.

7  Cover the back of the felt in
glue and stick on the backing felt.
Leave to dry.

8  Stick on the brooch back
using strong glue.

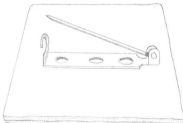

# VELVET JESTER HAT

## MADELAINE MILLINGTON

*Techniques used: stumpwork, machine appliqué (see pages 84–85 and 88–90)*

> ✳ YOU WILL NEED ✳
> *Lightweight cotton velvets, 75cm (30in) squares of pink and yellow and 20cm (8in) squares of green*
> *Gold metallic thread*
> *Cord*

1  Cut out one yellow and two pink pieces of velvet each 46cm (18 ¹/₂ in) x head measurement plus 2cm (³/₄ in) to allow for the upturn. Take into account that velvet is thick so make the measurement by doubling the material round your head.

2  Machine embroider circles with lines radiating from them on one piece of pink velvet. Cut out the centres and with an embroidery needle and metallic thread make random spiderweb stitches.

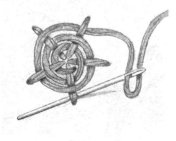

3  Place the embroidered pink velvet on top of the plain pink velvet, with right sides facing up. Then place the yellow velvet on the pink, with right sides facing together. Pin in place. Divide the head circumference into 18 equal 'fingers' and mark the lines, making them 15cm (6in) long. Machine down them, though not along the edge of the velvet as you will need these seams open for turning the hat the right way round. Cut between the stitched lines and clip into the corners.

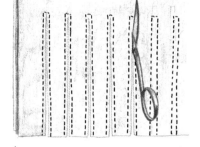

4  Reverse the shape and pull the fingers through so they are the right way round. Open the hat out and with the right sides facing sew up the back seam.

5  Turn the bottom of hat up by 6cm (2 ¹/₂ in) to reveal the yellow. Neaten the edge and stitch the upturn to the hat to stop it from falling down.

6  Using the stumpwork technique (see pages 84–85), make jester pictures. Apply these to the yellow band. In addition, you could sew bands of colour between the pictures.

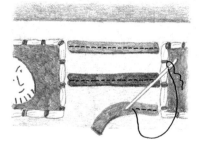

7  To make the hat ties, on the back of the green velvet mark at even intervals six rows of six eyelets. To make each eyelet, free machine a circle of stitches and cut out the centre.

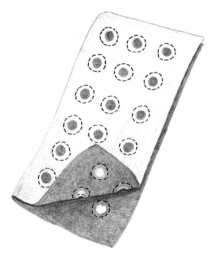

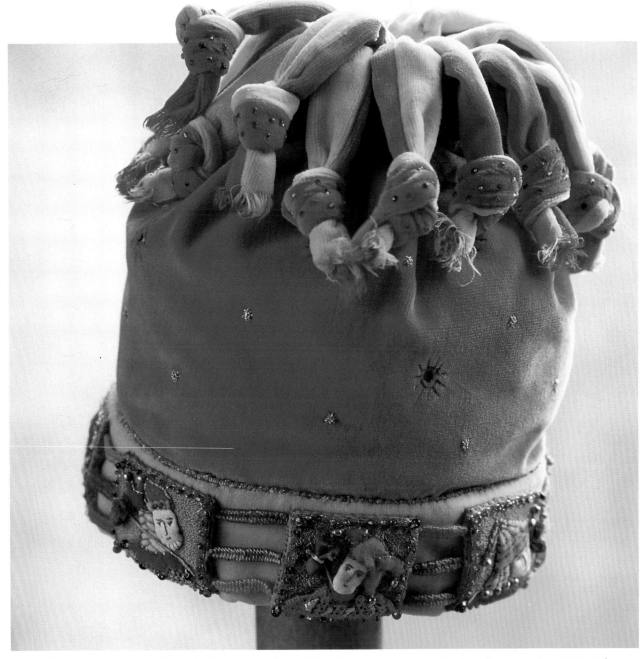

A hat for extroverts only. Pink and yellow cotton velvet with knotted velvet tassels sprouting from the crown are accompanied by stumpworked pictures around the brim.

8 Fold the green velvet in half with right sides facing and sew down the back seam. Turn it the right way round. Make or buy thin cord and thread through three rows of eyelets. Place a band over the fingers of the hat and pull the cord to fit the head. Tie the ends of the cord into a bow.

9 Knot the ends of the fingers and sew on decorative coloured beads.

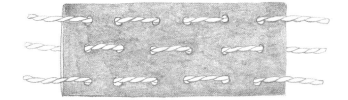

# FABRIC FLOWER BROOCH

## ABIGAIL MILL

*Techniques used: stumpwork, shadow appliqué (see pages 84-85 and 85-86)*

✳ YOU WILL NEED ✳

*Pencil and paper*
*20cm (8in) square of richly coloured thick felt*
*Scraps of silk, velvet and metallic organza*
*Metallic thread*
*Wadding*
*Brooch back*
*Needle and thread*

1 Draw a simple flower onto the paper. For a brooch, the flower should be about 10cm (4in) in diameter. This will be your template, so cut out the petals and centre individually. Pin onto the felt and cut out the petals and two centres.

2 Take one of the centres and layer small circles of silk, velvet and organza over the felt. Using hand stitching or a sewing machine, sew swirls over the circles to secure them onto the background and to define the pattern. Add details in metallic thread if you want to.

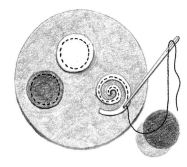

3 Lay a scrap of metallic organza over each petal and machine satin stitch around the edge, leaving a 5mm (¹/₅ in) allowance.

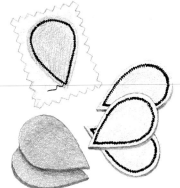

*Below:* The organza of this flower brooch has been satin stitched in place over the felt, and strips of bright fabrics have been machine and hand stitched on as details.

4  Tack each petal onto the back
of the appliquéd flower centre,
then take the second centre piece
and pin it onto the back, to cover
the join of the petals. Machine
around the centre, leaving a small
gap in the stitching.

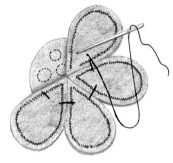

5  Stuff the flower centre with
the wadding to pad it out and
then sew up the opening.

6  Sew the brooch back onto the
centre back of the flower.

*Right:* A selection of brooches,
hair slides and earrings, all of various
sizes and all made in the same manner
as the flower brooch.

*Starry lampshade* illustrates the shadow and reverse appliqué techniques in organza and silk. Silk scraps are sandwiched together between layers of organza and bonded with fusible webbing. The top layer is then cut away at various points to reveal the silk beneath.

# STARRY LAMPSHADE
## KATE PEACOCK

***Techniques used: bonding, reverse appliqué (see pages 83 and 86-88)***

> ✳ YOU WILL NEED ✳
> *Wire lampshade frame with ring*
>     *at top and bottom*
> *Selection of habutai silk in*
>     *various colours*
> *2 long strips of silk organza*
>     *approximately 3 times the*
>     *circumference of the lower*
>     *ring*
> *Fusible webbing*
> *Needle and thread*
> *Craft knife*
> *Hole punch*

1  Cut the habutai silk pieces into star shapes.

2  Lay one of the large strips of silk organza on a flat surface and then lay a strip of webbing of the same size over it. Arrange the stars over the webbing at evenly spaced intervals.

3  Add small squares and triangles of silk to the stars that are scattered randomly around the webbing and lay contrasting coloured threads around the squares and stars.

4  Lay the other large strip of organza over the webbing to sandwich the silk pieces and webbing in between the two strips of organza. Iron the whole length so that everything is bonded together.

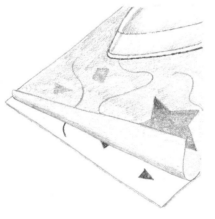

5  Cut through the top layer of organza around the stars and squares, to reveal the shapes below, and hand stitch around the shapes.

6  Hem the lower edge and fold over the top.

7  Pleat the shade, using an iron, and press down on the folds as if making a fan. On the inside fold of each pleat, punch a hole 2cm (³/₄ in) from the edge. These will be broken so that they can hook over the wire frame at the top.

# BLUE SILK BOOK

## KATE PEACOCK

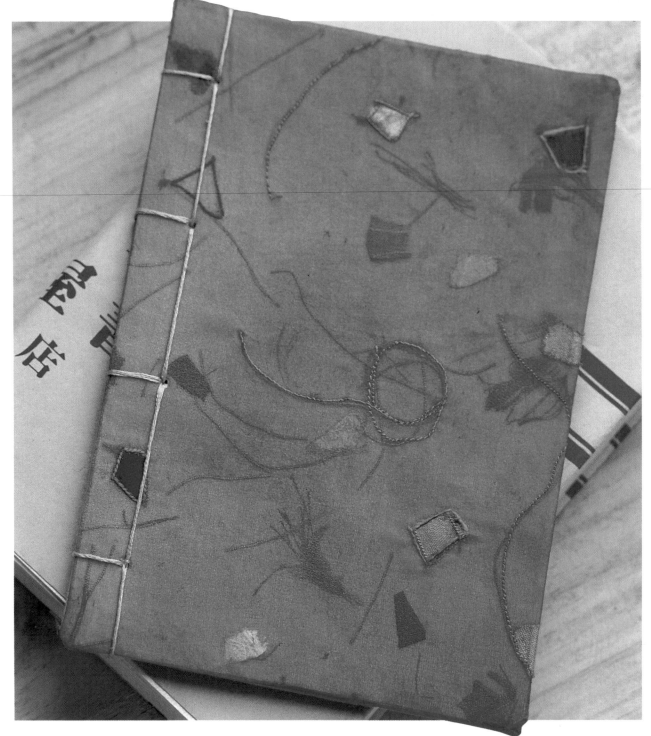

*Blue silk book* is reverse appliqué work stuck onto card to make a book cover.

*Techniques used: basic hand-stitched appliqué, bonding, reverse appliqué (see pages 81-82, 83 and 86-88)*

1  Cut the cartridge paper into sheets 3mm (¹/₁₀in) smaller than the card; these will be the pages of the book.

2  Lay the piece of silk chiffon on a flat surface and cover with layer of webbing. Place scraps of the habutai silk and the silk threads randomly on the webbing and cover with another layer of silk chiffon. Bond with a hot iron.

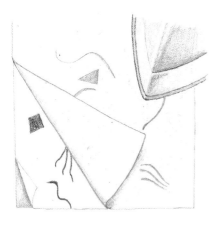

3  Cut away parts of the top layer of chiffon to reveal the shapes beneath. Then hand stitch or machine around the shapes.

4  Cover the card with rubber glue and stick onto the wrong side of the chiffon.

5  Glue round the edges of the back of the card and fold over the edges of the chiffon and stick down in place.

6  Glue one page of the book onto the back of the cover so that the raw edges of the chiffon are completely hidden.

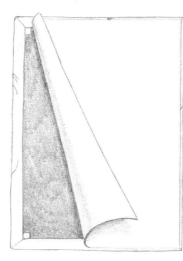

7  Repeat steps 2 to 6 for the other cover.

8  Put the pages between the front and the back covers and, using the bradawl, make four holes evenly spaced along the spine 2cm (³/₄in) from the edge.

9  Sew together with embroidery thread using blanket stitches. Using button thread, sew the covers and the pages together. The thread should be three times the length of the book plus 30cm (12in). Sew from one end of the book to the other using a running stitch. When this is done, take the thread over the spine and come back through the same hole. Make a stitch at right angles to each running stitch.

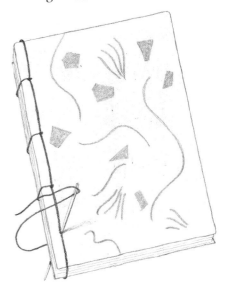

# ALL-SEEING HANDS SCARF

## FREDDIE ROBINS

*Techniques used: basic hand-stitched appliqué, machine appliqué (see pages 81-82 and 88-90)*

✳ YOU WILL NEED ✳
*Plain black woollen scarf,
    ideally 30cm (12in) wide
Paper and pencil
Marker pen
Green felt, enough for two hands
Red, white, orange and purple
    felt or blanket material,
    enough for two hands, four
    eyes and irises and a heart
Craft knife
Cutting board
Needle and black and red thick
    yarn*

1 Draw a hand shape onto paper and cut it out. Use this template to make two hands from the green felt and one each from the red and orange felts, giving you four hands in total.

2 Draw a heart shape in the middle of the template and cut the heart out. Pin the template onto one of the green hands and draw around the heart. Using the craft knife on the cutting board, cut out the heart.

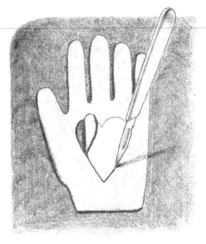

3 Draw the eye shape and circle on paper, then cut out and draw around the eye onto the white felt. Repeat until you have four eyes. For the irises, cut out four circles in different colours.

4 Machine the hand with the heart onto one end of the scarf.

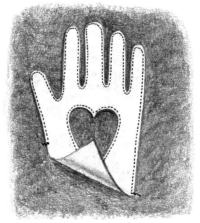

Sew black yarn into the centre of a circle, then sew the circle onto the eye and sew the eye into the centre of the heart.

5 Cut the red yarn into 1cm (1/2 in) long pieces and arrange around the heart. Stitch onto the scarf using a small over stitch and matching thread.

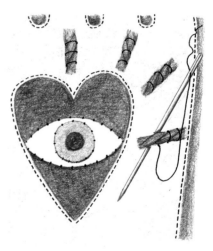

6 Work using different colour combinations for each hand. Sew black yarn into the centre of each remaining circle, then sew the circles into each remaining eye shape. Sew the eye onto the centre of the hand.

7 Cut the black yarn into 1cm (1/2 in) long pieces and arrange above each eye like eyelashes.

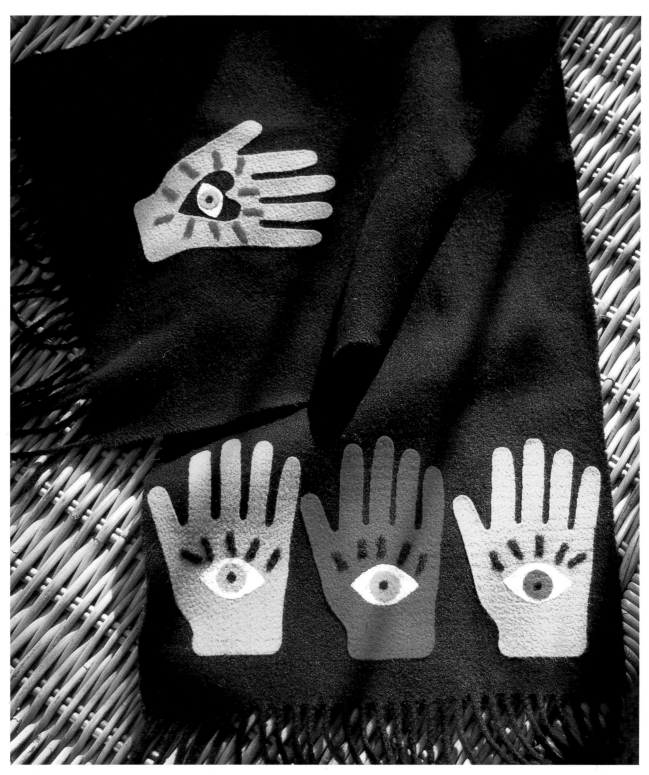

*All-seeing hands scarf* is an illustration of how successfully a shop-bought scarf can be turned into an individual and bright accessory. Shawls, throws and blankets can all be upgraded in this way. Felt is the ideal material to use as an appliqué fabric onto wool.

Stitch the eyelashes onto the hands, using a small over stitch and matching thread.

8 Arrange the three remaining hands on the other side of the scarf in a row. Machine in place.

9 Hand wash the scarf so that the appliqué motifs are held even more securely.

*Floating leaves and bunting blanket* is actually made up of three pieces, which makes decorating it much easier.
Each piece is appliquéd before being sewn together with a figure of eight stitch.

# FLOATING LEAVES AND BUNTING BLANKET

## LISA VAUGHAN

*Techniques used: basic hand-stitched appliqué, machine appliqué (see pages 81–82 and 88–90)*

> ✳ YOU WILL NEED ✳
> *Paper and pencil*
> *Blanket fabric, enough for the*
> *finished size you want plus*
> *the shapes to be sewn on (you*
> *can buy this as a blanket or*
> *buy pieces of woollen fabric;*
> *either buy different colours*
> *or dye them )*
> *Darning needle*
> *Selection of wools and cottons*

1  Cut out the blanket material into three equal strips.

2  Draw the shapes you require, transfer the design to card to make a template, and cut out the pieces from the blanket material.

3  Place the pieces on the blanket strips and arrange as you wish. Pin and then sew into position using blanket stitch in contrasting colours.

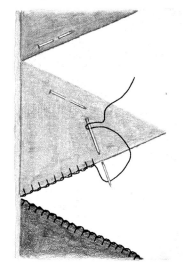

4  Sew the three strips of blanket together using a figure of eight stitch along the join.

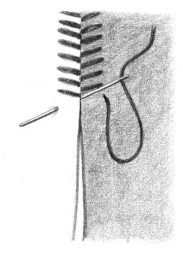

5  Couch detail in the form of swirls onto the design using a brightly coloured yarn.

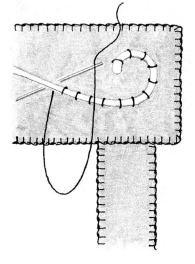

6  Sew running stitches diagonally along the chair seat, first in one direction and then the other, to produce a criss-cross pattern.

7  Blanket stitch around the outside edges.

# AIRMAIL PILLOWCASE

## LISA VAUGHAN

*Techniques used: basic hand-stitched appliqué, machine appliqué (see pages 81–82 and 88–90)*

✳ Y O U   W I L L   N E E D ✳

*Shirt fabric or cotton sheeting, about 100 x 80cm (40 x 32in) for the front, back and strip of an average pillowcase*
*Fabric scraps of your choice*
*Indelible pen*
*Beads*
*Buttons*
*Needle and coloured threads*

1  Cut out the front of the pillow-case to the desired size (75 x 45cm (30 x 18in) on average).

2  Cut the fabric scraps into the required shapes and arrange them on the front of the case and pin into position.

3  Machine and apply hand-stitching details.

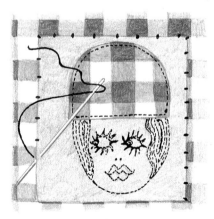

4  Apply the writing in either machine embroidery, hand stitching or indelible pen.

5  Sew on the beads. When making the salt packet, appliqué the square of material onto the pillowcase, leaving a small opening at one end. Fill the square with beads and then sew up the opening.

6  Cut out the back of the pillowcase so that it is 12.5cm (5in) larger than the front all the way around. To make up the pillowcase, mitre the corners on the wrong side of the back piece and then turn it the right way round. Push the corners right out, turn under the raw edges and press.

7  Place the top piece of the pillowcase under the turned edges of the back piece, then pin and sew around three sides, leaving one short end open. Hem under the raw edges of the opening.

8  Cut out a strip of material, the length of the pillowcase plus 2.5cm (1in) and 8cm (3in) wide.

9  Sew this strip lengthwise across the centre back of the pillowcase, allowing it to overlap the front edges of the pillowcase. Stitch down the overlap.

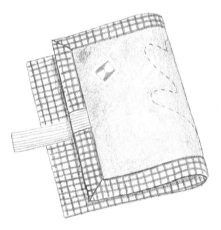

10  To make the hands, cut two pieces of cotton for each hand and sew together. Turn through and machine. Add a buttonhole to the centre of each hand.

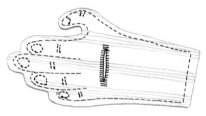

11  Hand stitch details in various colours onto the edge of the pillow-case and sew the buttons on place.

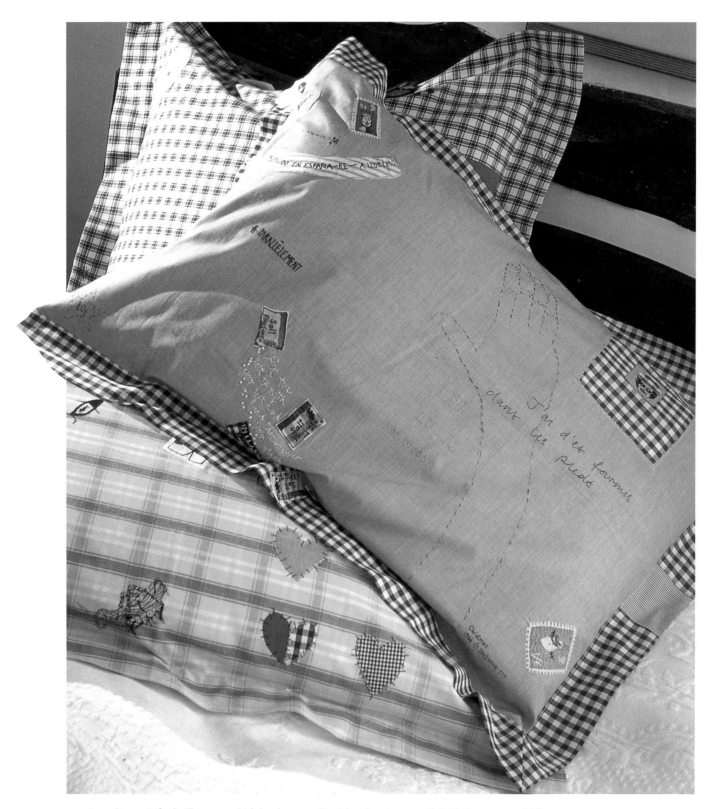

*Airmail* is an Oxford pillowcase which has been appliquéd with various motifs, including pieces of fabric cut out to represent stamps and a tiny patch filled with beads and made to look like a salt packet.

# JAMBOREE BUTTONS

## NANCY NICHOLSON

*Techniques used: bonding, machine appliqué (see pages 83 and 88-90)*

✳ YOU WILL NEED ✳
*Shop-bought buttons to cover with snap-on back*
*Fusible webbing*
*Scraps of green and purple silk*
*12cm (5in) square of muslin*

1 Work on a set of buttons together. Iron the webbing onto the colour silk you want your buttons to be (purple in this instance). This will be the colour of your buttons. Then iron this onto a large piece of muslin. This is used to guide the buttons under the sewing machine.

2 When you buy the buttons, buy ones that are stitched onto a piece of card and use this card with the buttons in position, to make a template. Draw around the template onto the webbing.

3 Iron the contrasting green silk onto the webbing, then draw the leaf motif on the paper backing. Cut out, remove the paper and iron the motif onto the circle of purple silk.

4 Embroider around the leaf motif, using the sewing machine embroidery foot attachment. This can be done by hand if preferred.

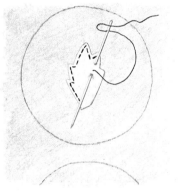

5 Cut out the circles of silk from the muslin and running stitch around the outer edge, as close to the edge as possible, leaving enough thread to pull so that the thread can be gathered.

6 Draw in the thread over button front. Snap on the button back and snip off any excess threads.

*Above and right:* Delicate silk-covered buttons such as these *Jamboree buttons* are in fact easier to make than they look because you can buy buttons ready to cover from most haberdashers.

# POP ART BAG
## KATE PEACOCK

*Techniques used: bonding, machine appliqué (see pages 83 and 88–90)*

---

**✳ YOU WILL NEED ✳**
*75cm (30in) square of fabric for the bag*
*75cm (30in) square of fusible webbing*
*Scraps of silk*
*Silk organza*
*Paper and pencil*

---

1 Lay the fabric on a flat surface and place webbing of the same size over it. Then place the silk scraps randomly over the webbing and then a layer of silk organza.

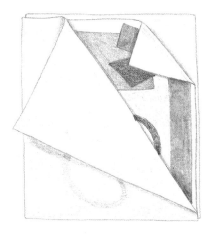

2 Bond everything together using a warm iron.

3 Repeat these steps for the back of the bag.

4 Make a paper template of the shape you want the bag to be. Place a plain piece of lining fabric on the right side of the design and then pin the paper template onto it in position.

5 Sew around the edge of template, securing it, the lining and the appliquéd fabric together. Leave an opening at the bottom so that the bag can be turned the right way round. Do this for the back and the front of the bag.

6 Trim off any excess material from the seam joining the template, lining and appliquéd fabric. Turn inside out and press flat. Machine along the lower edge to close the opening.

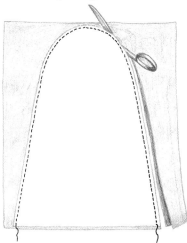

7 To form the gusset, cut a strip of fabric 9cm (3 ³/₄ in) wide and the length of the two sides and the bottom of the bag. Fold in the seam allowance along the gusset strip and sew the strip on the outside so that it is between the front and back of the bag.

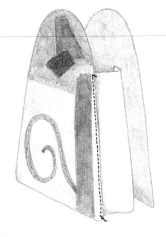

8 For the handles, make a large D-shaped template to the required size. Pin the template onto one side of the bag where you want the handles to be. Sew around the template in satin stitch. Repeat on the other side.

9 With care, cut away the inside of the D shapes.

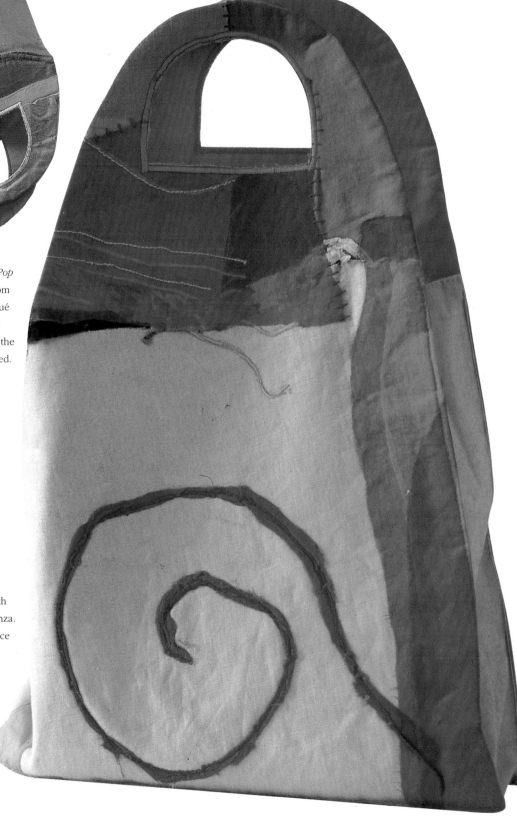

*Above:* The reverse side of the *Pop Art bag* shows scraps of silk from the shadow and reverse appliqué work. The satin stitch on the handles gives a bold contrast to the delicacy of the silk materials used.

*Right: Pop Art bag* is made with thick embroidery silks and organza. The handles are secured in place with satin stitch.

# GINGHAM FISH CUSHION
## HELEN MUSSELWHITE

The appliquéd pieces of this *Gingham fish cushion* have been bonded in place with fusible webbing then further secured with large irregular hand stitches to make this simple composition.

*Techniques used: basic hand-stitched appliqué, bonding, machine appliqué (see pages 81-82, 83 and 88-90)*

1  Draw the parts of a fish and other shapes – a body, half body, fins, tails, eyes, iris and heart – and cut out in card to use as a template.

2  Iron the webbing onto the back of the gingham to be used for the shapes and then cut out the hearts, iris and fin. Cut the fish body, the half body, eye and other fins from the felt.

3  Pin the felt fish into the centre of one of the calico squares and machine all around the edge. Once the main body is down, pin and then machine the felt half body, the felt fins and the eye.

4  Place the gingham iris on the felt eye, the large heart in the middle of the fish and the fin detail at the end. Place the other hearts at each corner. Machine in place. Because the gingham is backed with webbing, there is no need to turn the edges under. Using the embroidery silk, sew large hand stitches around the hearts.

5  Sew in a mouth and large running stitch all around the edge of the calico square, leaving a seam allowance.

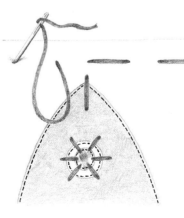

6  Sew the calico appliquéd square centrally onto the gingham. Turn under the edges and machine stitch close to the edge all the way round. Then, using the two other calico pieces for the back, make up a cushion with a back centre opening, taking seam allowances of 1.5cm (⅝in).

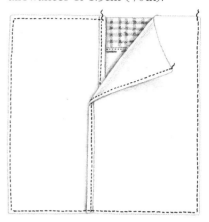

7  Cut a zigzag pattern along one side of each of the four blue felt strips in order to form four triangular shapes.

8  Pin two felt strips together and sew around the zigzag side, leaving the straight side open. Stuff the zigzags with wadding and then pin one strip onto the top edge of the cushion and the other onto the lower edge.

9  Sew the pompoms onto the tips of each triangle.

# PICTURE BLANKET

## KIRSTEN WATTS

*Techniques used: basic hand-stitched appliqué, bonding, machine appliqué (see pages 81-82, 83 and 88-90)*

✳ YOU WILL NEED ✳

*Paper and pencil*
*Acetate sheets*
*Felt tip pen*
*Printing screens (optional)*
*Polythene sheet*
*Old towel and teatowel*
*Sheet of calico*
*Masking tape*
*2.5cm (1in) double-sided tape*
*Blanket the size of your choice*
*G-clamp*
*Selection of dyes*
*Fake fur*
*Scraps of woollen fabrics*
*Fusible webbing*

1 Draw your design on paper and photocopy the images and writing, if there is any, onto acetate sheets. Touch them up with a black felt tip pen.

2 Take the acetate sheets and the printing screens to a printer who can expose the images and writing onto your screens to make iron-on stencils. Use one screen for the writing and another for the smaller images.

3 If you have access to a screen printer, follow steps 3–7, otherwise just paint on the fabric dye with a brush or stitch on areas of felt. Fix the polythene sheet onto your table with masking tape. Fold an old towel and tape that over the polythene, then tape the calico over the old towel.

4 Once this is done, place the double-sided tape all around the table. Now lay the blanket over everything and stick it onto the table. If it needs further securing, pin it down.

If you need a template on which to base the picture blanket, enlarge the line drawing on a photocopier.

5 Cut out the stencil and iron into position on the blanket. Iron-on stencils mean that you can block out areas that you don't want to print.

6 Use the G-clamp to secure the screen to the table. Spoon your chosen dye colours generously along the top edge of the screen. Pull the squeegee of the screen through the dye towards you. Ensure that you press the dye evenly along the screen.

7 To dye smaller areas, turn the screen upside down and mask off with paper and masking tape. This will allow a small amount of dye to come through.

The design for this decorative and unusual blanket is created using photocopied images that are transformed into iron-on stencils.

8  Wash the screens in cold water and once the blanket is dry, peel off the stencils. The blanket will have to be steamed to fix the dyes. (Your local college with a textiles department will have steaming facilities.)

9  After the blanket has been steamed, wash it in cold water and then in warm water with detergent until the water runs clear. Leave to dry for a day.

10  The blanket is now ready to be appliquéd with fabrics of your choice. Here, fake fur and wools were used. Iron the webbing onto the back of the fabrics. Draw the shapes onto the back of the webbing, cut them out and peel off the backing.

11  Place each piece in position and press carefully. Use a tea towel between the blanket and the fake fur when ironing and fixing the webbing.

12  Stitch the motifs into position either by hand, using running or blanket stitches, or by machine.

These *Ethnic by design* bags are sewn from hand-made
wool felt dyed white, black or dark brown. A fairly complicated pattern
has been cut by using inlay and reverse inlay techniques to create two images –
one positive, the other negative. Each has been edged and handled with pure silk thread.

# ETHNIC BY DESIGN BAG

## ANNE MORGAN

**Techniques used: inlay work (see pages 90-93)**

---

**✳ YOU WILL NEED ✳**

*Plain and tracing paper and pencil*

*Card*

*2 pieces of dark brown wool felt 66 x 35cm (about 26¹/₂ x 14in)*

*2 pieces of cream wool felt 66 x 35cm (about 26¹/₂ x 14in)*

*Tailor's chalk*

*Craft knife*

*Cutting board*

*Embroidery needle*

*Pure silk thread - thin and thick, cream and brown*

*Dark brown and cream silk for lining 66 x 35cm (about 26¹/₂ x 14in)*

*Braid*

---

1  Draw your design on paper, marking clearly where it should be dark and light. Trace the drawing and transfer it onto card to use as a template.

2  Pin one piece of each colour of felt together. Position the templates and draw around them in pen or tailor's chalk. Pin both pieces onto the cutting board and, using a craft knife, cut through them both.

3  Separate the felts and place each on a flat surface. Remove cream shapes from the cream cut felt and replace with the brown shapes. Then replace the cream shapes onto the brown cut felt.

4  Pin the inserted pieces onto the background felt, trimming away any excess to make an exact fit. Using small slip stitch, sew the pieces down.

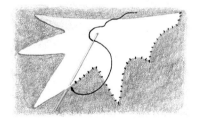

5  Using the photograph as a guide, stitch borders along the appliquéd pieces with silk thread.

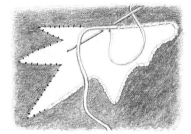

6  Cut a piece of cream silk slightly smaller than the felt. Turn under the edges and hand stitch onto the back of the appliqué work, to act as a lining. Repeat with the brown silk.

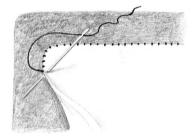

7  Fold the piece over twice, 27cm (10 ³/₄ in) from each end to form an envelope-shaped bag. Using a sewing machine sew down the sides, then sew braid over the machine stitching and carry it on to form a handle, stitching the braids together at the top. Sew on two buttons and loops for the fastenings.

# FURTHER READING

❋

Adler, Peter, and Barnard, Nicholas, *Asafo African Flags of the Fante*, Thames and Hudson, 1992

Baird, Ljilana, *Quilts*, Museum Quilts Publications, 1994

Bawden, Juliet, *The Art and Craft of Appliqué*, Mitchell Beazley, 1991

Beck, Thomasina, *The Embroiderer's Story*, David and Charles, 1995

Betterton, Sheila, *More Quilts and Coverlets from The American Museum in Britain*, The American Museum in Britain

Hulbert, Anne, *Folk Art Quilts*, Anaya, 1992

King, Donald, and Levy, Santina, *The Victoria and Albert Museum's Textile Collection: Embroideries in Britain from 1200–1750*, Victoria and Albert Museum, 1993

Puls, Hert, *Textiles of the Kuna Indians of Panama*, Shire Publications, 1988

Tucker, Dorothy, and Best, Muriel, and Lugg, Vicky, *Needlework School*, Quarto, 1989

# ARTISTS AND STOCKISTS

❋

The artists and designers featured in this book have kindly agreed that their addresses be included. Many of them give lectures and run courses or hold workshops on the art of appliqué, supply the necessary equipment and undertake commissions, both private and public. Write to them, enclosing a large stamped addressed envelope, for further details. International reply coupons, available from post offices, should be sent to overseas artists and designers.

**ARTISTS**

**Petra Boase**
46 Portobello Road
London W11
tel: 0171 221 7435

**Jane Bristow**
225 Hulme Street
Hulme
Manchester M15 5EF
tel: 0161 226 5483

**Jane Burch Cochran**
6830 Rabbit Hash Hill Road
Rabbit Hash
KY 41005, USA
tel: 001 606 586 9143

**Jo Cranston**
Cross Street Studios
14 Cross Street,
Hove
East Sussex BN3 AJ
tel: 01273 725321;
fax: 01273 746411

**Belinda Downes**
Waalstraat 77, 3rd floor
1079 DR Amsterdam
The Netherlands
tel/fax: 00 31 20 646 0045

**Nancy N. Erickson**
3250 Patte Canyon Road

Missoula
MO 59803-1703
USA
tel: 001 406 5494671

**Deborah Gonet**
207B Chevening Road
Queens Park
London NW6 6DT
tel/fax: 0181 968 7481

**Rachael Howard**
14 Groombridge Road
London E9 7DP
tel/fax: 0181 986 9889

**Barbara Jepson**
9 Greenside
Ainsworth
Near Bolton
Lancashire BL2 5SE
tel: 01204 384514

**Natasha Kerr**
Unit W11, Cockpit Workshops
Northington Street
London WC1N 2NP
tel: 0171 916 4640

**Abigail Mill**
Studio 10, Muspole Workshop
25-7 Muspole Street
Norwich
Norfolk NR3 1DJ
tel: 01603 760955

**Madelaine Millington**
5 Cathedral Close
Guildford
Surrey GU2 5TL
tel: 01483 31693

**Anne Morgan**
183 Hayfield Road
Birch Vale
Stockport SK12 5DA
tel: 01663 743840

**Helen Musselwhite**
Unit 9, Goosey Wick Farm
Charney Bassett
Wantage
Oxfordshire OX12 OEY
tel: 01367 718778

**Nancy Nicholson**
The Ark
Goddards Green Road
Benenden
Cranbrook, Kent
tel: 01580 240948

**Kate Peacock**
85 Eaton Rise
Eaton College Road
London NW3 2DB
tel: 0171 483 1686

**Freddie Robins**
Unit W8, Cockpit Yard Workshops
Northington Street
London WC1N 2NP
tel: 0171 916 6447;
fax: 0171 916 2455

**Jane A. Sassaman**
1927 West Barry
Chicago
IL 60657
USA
tel: 001 312 248 3659

**Robin Schwalb**
75 Livingston Street 11B
Brooklyn
NY 11201
USA
tel: 001 718 797 0129

**Hayley Smith**
11 Worcester Close
Braintree
Essex CM7 1EH
tel: 01376 327628

**Lisa Vaughan**
Unit 228
Highbury Workshops
Aberdeen House
22 Highbury Grove
London N5 2EA
tel: 0171 359 4073

**Kirsten Watts**
7 High Bank
Langdon Hills
Basildon
Essex SS16 6TG
tel: 01268 410375

## STOCKISTS

*Australia and New Zealand*
**Nancy's Embroidery Ltd**
326 Tinakori Road
PO Box 245
Thorndon
Wellington
New Zealand

**Altamira**
34 Murphy Street
South Yarra
Melbourne
Victoria 3141
Australia

*Canada*
**Jet Handicraft Studio Ltd**
1847 Marine Drive West
Vancouver, BC V7V 1J7
Canada

*UK*
**Silken Strands**
Rosemary Irving Mail Order
33 Linksway Gatley
Cheadle
Cheshire SK8 4LA
tel: 0161 426 9108
*(specialist embroidery threads and fabrics)*

**DMC Creative World Ltd**
Tel 0116 2811040
*(sewing and embroidery threads)*

**Fred Aldous**
PO Box 37
Lever Street
Manchester M60 1UX
tel: 0161 236 2477
*(most craft materials)*

**Creative Beadcraft Ltd**
Denmark Works
Sheepcote Dell Road
Beaumont End
Near Amersham
Bucks HP7 0RX
tel: 01494 715606

*USA*
**Handicraft from Europe**
PO Box 31524
San Francisco, CA 94131-02524
USA

**Needleworks Ltd**
4041 Tulane Avenue
New Orleans, LA 70119
USA

# INDEX

\*

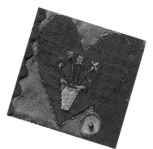